UNDER THE WEEPING Willow Tree

A Memoir about Grief, Loss and Disability

UNDER THE WEEPING
Willow Tree

A Memoir about Grief, Loss and Disability

Linda S. Madison, MSW

Under the Weeping Willow Tree

Printed in the United States of America
ISBN 979-8-3302-3229-1 (sc)
ISBN 979-8-3302-3230-7 (e)

06 / 07 / 2024

This book is printed on acid-free paper.

Pro Creation Press
www.procreationpress.com

In Memory of

My Beloved Daughter

Cara Lynee Reyes

March 21, 1970 – October 7, 2021

My Beloved Mother

Earleen Parrott

March 10, 1918 – February 27, 1953

DEDICATED

To
My Children

Cara, Phillip, Rebecca, and Elena

For giving me love, courage, and strength.

ACKNOWLEDGEMENTS

To God be the Glory

To Dr. Chris Carver:

For knowing where his strength comes from; for understanding, caring for, and saving my life.

To Shayne Mathews, my first grandchild,

Who was born the day after my surgery and gave me the determination to fight to live.

To my stepmother, Dorothy Parrott.

Who unselfishly took me in and raised me to the best of her ability.

To my children, Cara, Phillip, Rebecca, and Alena.

For healing me with your love and making me a deserving mother.

To my sister, Marsha Vargo.

For being close to my heart.

To Fred Simpson.

For loving and supporting me in everything I do.

To my brother, Jimmy Parrott.

For giving me strength and encouragement to know I could do it.

To Ruben Mendoza.

For being there for the children.

To Lupe Tune.

For your friendship and love.

To my friend Suzanne Cagle.

For being a true friend to me and accepting me for who I have become.

To Dan Petersen, my college English teacher.

For making me know the love of writing with heart.

To Roma guy, my SFSU supervisor

For giving me the chance to prove myself.

To Dr. Don Williams.

For supporting me and helping me through my recovery.

To all the people who have given me their love, thoughts, feelings, and hearts. No one is forgotten.

Bio

Linda Madison was born in Gary, Indiana. As a child, she lived in the same home from 5 years old until she left to become married at 19. Linda's music is her first love. An accomplished pianist, she has played for many choirs and weddings and performed before audiences. Her survival skills were many as she crossed into motherhood at the age of 21. Raising four children as a single mother at age 42, the tragic event of brain surgery changed her lives.

Two years after her surgery, she passionately devoted her time to an organization she founded and directed in 1992 called the *Central Coast Impairment Management Program (CCIMP).* This organization provided services to brain injury survivors and their families, giving them resources, referrals, and peer support regarding disability. As this program grew, physicians began to ask for support in developing groups for their clients with dialysis, multiple sclerosis, arthritis, and hearing impairment.

As this program became successful, Linda returned to college to receive her BA and her Masters in Social Work at California State University, Fresno, and San Francisco State University. Sitting on various committees, Linda was the representative for staff and faculty with disabilities. She launched and developed the *Disability Action, Education, and Representation Program (DEAR),* giving education to students on acceptance of themselves as unique individuals and addressing ADA compliance issues on campus.

Linda won the 2000-2001 CSU STAR AWARD for San Francisco State University (Students That Are Recognized for Outstanding Leadership) and was speaker and pianist for her 2001 Bachelor's graduation at San Francisco State University and pianist for her Masters at California State University Fresno.

While doing her Masters of Social Work at California State University, Fresno, Linda founded and *directed the Professional Business Women and Men with Disabilities (PBWMD),* an organization that gave support to professional women and men throughout the university and Fresno, giving them information, support, advocacy, and resources. This program gave advocacy to other college students who were disabled.

TABLE OF CONTENTS

PREFACE

This book is not a finished product. It was a means by which I wanted to leave my children with praise for their courage, selfishness, and unfailing love. I also wanted to reach out to other women who have survived grief, loss, and disability. I wanted them to know that grief and loss are only for a season, but joy comes in the morning. Despite the resistance we, as women with disabilities, receive in every aspect of our lives, we can derive great courage and learn who we are through our grief and loss. Disability is dying to the old and learning to live with the new person we have become. Facing that reality, I call it "the circle of acceptance," which means we accept who they are for their unique individuality. Yes, it takes courage, and it is a risk. You are vulnerable, and it will mean stepping out of your comfort zone. Rome was not built in a day, and this may take months or years, depending on how much you need to work on yourself. But it is worth the wait! Your reward will be greater than you have imagined.

The reader will know that I felt great pain at my loss. I also derived great victory from those of my friends, colleagues, and family who watched me blossom as I began to grow and accept who I had become. It will be apparent that love is the greatest attribute in assisting me to a life of acceptance. As I began to love others and be thankful for life itself, I began to feel the healing balm of love from those around me.

The identities of my family have not been concealed, as they were a vital part of my life and the woman, I have become today. . .

Linda S. Madison, MSW

CHAPTER I

A Place Called Heaven

Nestled beneath the weeping willow tree, I sat watching the branches sway back and forth in the wind. It was as if they were singing a gentle, comforting song just for me. The big willow with its long branches was my favorite place to play as a little girl. When I was hurt, afraid, or alone, I saw the willow as a place of refuge and solace. I had no idea that in the months to come, I would need the willow to fill the loneliness from the greatest loss I will ever experience.

It was morning, and Mommy lay in bed, motioning for me to come to her. "Hop up here in bed and let Mommy read you a story!"

Mommy was always in bed and sick most of the time. Daddy was the best dad ever. Cooking, cleaning, and caring for my mother after a hard day —his work never ended. My big sister Marsha looked after me when she was not in school. Although she was 12 years older, we were the best of friends.

While my sister washed the dishes, I stood motionless in the doorway of the kitchen as two men in white coats put my mother on a cart. I giggled, and my sister said "Linda, that is not funny!"

Well, what did a three-year-old know about hospitals, gurneys, and men in white coats? My days were filled with anticipation of my mother's coming home. I would sit on her lap at the hospital and eat from her plate as she smiled lovingly.

"Honey, eat all those mashed potatoes. Mommy does not want any of them!" she said to me as she peered over the white hospital sheets.

My nose pressed against the windowpane of my bedroom. I watched the weeping willow sing her song. The heart necklace that my mother gave me lay neatly by my bed. *"Why do I feel so lonely, and where is mommy?"*

"Hi Button Nose!" Grandpa Conley, my mother's father, said as I jumped on his lap. I loved Grandpa. A big man, he was gentle and loving. As long as I can remember where Grandpa was, Grandma was there too.

"Grandpa, where is Mommy? I miss her! When is she coming home"?

Grandpa's gentle eyes looked very sad and concerned. "Why, honey, Mommy is gone to heaven!" "Oh," I said. Finally, someone gave me an answer! *Mommy must like heaven; she's been gone a very long time.*

My father planned a trip to go see my uncle Ben and aunt Grace in Denver, Colorado. The airplane was so big, and I squirmed nervously while sitting next to Daddy.

"What's wrong, sweetie?" Daddy said.

"I am hot, Daddy! Can I open a window and throw out my dolly?"

"Nope, we will be there in no time! Just sit still and look at the pretty blue sky."

Six months had passed since my mommy had gone away. As I look back, I can only imagine the pain my father was feeling from the loss of my mother. There was never a hint that anything was wrong, and I believe that my father was sparing those feelings to shield me from hurt.

This trip lasted two weeks. Returning home, my thoughts turned once again to missing my mother. After being tucked into bed, I would hear whispered words as the family sat and talked for what seemed like hours. As I drifted off to sleep, I sensed my father would come and kiss me goodnight before going to bed. "Sweet dreams, honey," he said.

As a child of 4, I had memories of housekeepers with strange accents and long dresses with big black shoes. One was named Rose. This was her second time taking care of me, and she seemed happy to have the job. As she pinched my cheek, her eyes would twinkle, and her teeth were big and yellow. "Look at those rosy cheeks; look at that curly hair—since I have been here," she would say.

There were many women in our house who took care of me after Rose. Some were good, and some weren't. These women made me miss my mom even more.

Even though he put in long hours at work, my father was always sure to bring me something special when he got home. Meeting him at the door was the biggest part of my day. "Hi Daddy! What have you got for me today?" His big arms engulfed me as he threw me in the air and caught me.

"How's my big girl?"

I giggled with glee. "I am so happy you are home!"

I missed Daddy when he was gone to work. The days were long and sometimes boring. During the day, I would sneak out and playfully visit the neighbors. I would walk blocks and blocks without knowing where I was. One day, on one of my little walks, I decided to knock on a neighbor's door.

"Linda!" she exclaimed! "You are too far from home! Let me walk you back to your house!"

When I was returned safely, the housekeeper did not even know I had been gone. The neighbor told her, "Do you have any idea how long this child has been gone, and how long has it been since she had a bath or her hair has been washed?"

When Daddy came home that night, I could hear the raised voices in the next room again. They were not happy voices. The next thing I knew, there was a new housekeeper taking care of me.

"Where is my sister?" I asked one day. I did not know she went to live with Grandma and Grandpa. I guess all this was just too much for my father to handle. After all, she was a teenager, and you know how teenagers can be! I later found out that she had no choice in the matter.

"She is living here with Grandpa," told me.

"But I miss sister," I insisted. I could tell everyone was being secretive about what was going on. The following year after my mother's death seemed endless. My father worked so much that I can hardly remember seeing him. Every Sunday, we had dinner at Grandma's house. I could see my sister and eat Grandma's fried chicken, mashed potatoes, gravy, biscuits, and a hot apple pie made with apples from the big tree in the backyard. Walking in the orchard with Grandpa, Grandma, and me, we would look for the apples on the big tree. "Pick them up while the pickings are good!" Grandpa would shout.

And plop! They would fall right into Grandma's big apron. Those were very special days for me. I felt safe and secure with Grandma and Grandpa and, most of all, very much loved. My memories of my grandparents were the best of all. There was no doubt that they loved and cared about me very much.

As the days and months passed, memories of my loving mother began to fade. I returned to my special place under the big willow. Its branches had grown longer, and I was growing taller. My special friend, Danny Boy, from next door, would keep me company, and I was occupied most of the time.

"Linda, come here!" he would say. I would jump right in the big old washtub, and he would pour buckets of water over my head as we screamed with joy! We would romp and play for hours on end. Danny Boy was quite a guy and lots of fun to be around.

Things around our house were pretty normal, except Daddy was not home as much. When he was, he was always arguing with me.

"Now, honey, do you see this paper on the floor? You just squat and poop and call me when you are done!"

I was having a difficult time managing my own needs, and my father was trying as a last resort. No matter how much or how long I tried sitting on the potty, I could not have a bowel movement. By the time I went, it was painful and difficult. I avoided the bathroom for days, sometimes a week at a time. In the fifties, no one knew about the disorder that children can acquire after a traumatic event. It is called encopresis. With this disorder, elimination becomes very difficult, and severe constipation becomes a serious problem. I went through a lot of shame and blame for this. No one seemed to know or realize that I had been traumatized by losing my mother and needed help. Of course, I had to deal with a lot of enemas. Twenty-five years of psychotherapy resolved this issue. The mind-body connection is very powerful.

I was 5 years old and wondering why I had not seen Daddy very much lately. I found out why he was so busy.

"Linda, we are going on a little trip!" he told me one day. "Okay, daddy, why?"

"There is someone I want you to meet." I guess we wouldn't be gone too long because we hardly packed anything. In the car, Daddy was very quiet and intense as he drove, flipping the radio off and on every few minutes. After a three-hour drive, the car reached a screeching halt.

"We here?"

"Certainly, honey; hop out!" When Daddy rang the doorbell, a very attractive woman with a big smile answered it.

"Hi Sam, come on in! Who is this?"

"This is my little girl, Linda." Linda, this is Dorothy." Smiling shyly, I said, "Hi!"

It was obvious that Daddy and Dorothy liked being alone. I really did not know what was going on, but I knew I liked her very much. Looking for anyone who might fill the empty place that my mommy filled, I welcomed her with open arms. Actually, I found myself sitting right smack dab in the middle of her lap!

"Ohhhhhhhh." She said. "You're a big girl!"

I really was a big girl, because now the family thought food was a good cure for me missing my mommy; I got all the cookies, candy, cakes, and pies I ever wanted. The only problem was that I was well over 15 pounds over my normal weight. Daddy gave me a disapproving look, and I started to hop off.

"No," Dorothy said. "You sit right here on my lap and talk to me!"

That was the beginning of a very special relationship between Dorothy and me.

While I shivered on the couch one day in Grandma's living room, I waited to hear from my father. I was very sick and was told that I had what they called "pneumonia."

"What?" I said, "poomonia?"

"Yes," Grandma told me. "You must rest and get well soon so you can see your dad and Dorothy when they come back."

"Grandma, where did they go?"

"Why, honey, they've gone to get married! You were to be the flower girl, but you were too sick." "Grandma, who is married?" I asked, "And what is a flower girl?"

Grandma attempted to tell me. "Well, you see, when two people fall in love wa. . .Grandma's voice faded away as I fell asleep.

I stretched and yawned as I listened to Grandma moving back and forth in the kitchen, waking me up to the sound of singing birds and the sun peeking through the old house's shades. Every step she made was a creak, creak, creak! Standing by my bed suddenly, she held a tray with cereal, milk, and toast.

"Feeling better, honey?" she asked. I hope so, because your dad and Dorothy will be here any day.

I was not very hungry, but I was anxious to see my dad. I didn't want Grandma to think I was too sick to see them, so I took a piece of toast and put it under my pillow. *Now, she will think I ate it all!* I thought.

That was until I looked up and saw her watching me! Grandma smiled sweetly. "Honey, if you don't want to eat now, that is quite all right." Grandma was so forgiving; what would I do without her? She was my biological grandmother and had so many traits that reminded me of Mommy. I think that's why I liked being with her so much. It was like being right beside my mom.

About noon, I heard Grandma say, "Come right in. She is over here in the living room.

I could have jumped for joy, for that was my dad, and, sure enough, there was that nice lady named Dorothy!

CHAPTER II

Dorothy Was Her Name

The days were filled with excitement, and Dorothy was there most of the time with Daddy and me. Together, they were planning a big trip that would take place very soon!

"Dorothy, where are we going?" I asked.

She packed things very neatly in the suitcase as I watched very intently. "We are all going to Niagara Falls."

It really didn't matter where we were all going; I was just happy that we were going on the trip together.

"Grab the bags, Dorothy and Linda; you carry the night case," Daddy said.

The miles from Indiana to Niagara Falls seemed to last forever. I loved riding in the car because I got to sleep most of the way. It was like lying in Grandpa's arms while he rocked me in his big rocking chair. Reaching our destiny, my father unloaded the car.

Standing on the cliffs, I looked down upon the beautiful falls. They were so white and looked like big pillows of clouds falling from the sky. I was mesmerized by the loud noise the water made against the rocks.

"Linda, have a look at that one! Isn't it lovely?"

My father was so happy. I had not seen him smile so much for a very long time. "We are going to see some of our relatives, Linda; would you like that?"

"Sure, Daddy," I said. I did not realize that their relatives lived in Tennessee or even remember which ones we went to see, but I do know that our trip did not turn out like I would have liked it to.

It was a very hot, sunny day, and we had been traveling for quite a few hours before we reached the relative's house. Dorothy seemed very happy, always polite and smiling. This was her first time meeting the relatives, and everyone was very happy for my father. I think they were mostly happy that he had found someone to care for me. I didn't know or realize that this special trip was their honeymoon. It is unknown to me how Dorothy could have had so much patience and love when she had to share Daddy with me!

There was a large hill on the outside of the house. All the kids were running up and down the hill, trying to see who could run the fastest. Of course, I had to get into the action.

"Hey, Linda! Want to try? It's so much fun!" one of the cousins said.

"Sure, I can!" I said. Positioning my body at the top of the hill, I looked around. "*This is a pretty steep hill,*" I told myself.

I looked at the bottom of the hill to see if there was something to brace my body against. A few planks of wood stuck out from the porch, and a big refrigerator sat on top of them. That was it! I would run right into it and stop.

I started running. The further I ran, the faster I went. I was running out of breath, and I could feel the dirt slipping under my feet. I reached the plank, and as I did, my foot slipped and my leg went right under the plank, taking a big chunk of skin from my knee. I watched the skin as it flew up in the air. *"Oh!"* I thought as the pain began.

I began to cry, and everyone flew to my side. Lifting me up, Daddy carried me to the house and wrapped a sheet around my knee.

"Let's get her the doctor, Sam. It is bleeding pretty badly," Dorothy said.

The drive to the doctor seemed to last forever. By now, I was really hurting. The gash in my knee was about an inch long and deep. The blood was already seeping through the sheet. Finally, the car came to a screeching halt. Daddy carried me in and lifted me onto the table where the doctor examined my knee.

"Nasty cut! We will fix you right up!" he said. He was a nice man and made me feel like he knew what he was talking about. The shot he gave me was worse than the wound! My Daddy and Dorothy were appreciative of his help, and we started back to the relatives to pack for home.

Dorothy was making her way into my heart and our home. This was the first experience I had with her helping me through a childhood crisis. I felt at ease with the comfort she gave me, and I could tell Daddy liked her.

Home was peaceful, and my father started to work once again. Dorothy was a fine cook, and our house was full of the wonderful smells of apple pies, navy beans, and cornbread.

I was five-years-old. I still did not know of my biological mother's death or that this woman was about to be my stepmother.

Dorothy was a nice lady, but she was making herself awfully comfortable around my dad's house. She even sleeps in Daddy's room in his bed! *"Mommy won't like that when she comes home."*

Months passed, and I returned to my playtime rituals under the willow. "Hi Danny Boy! Come play with me!"

Danny stooped under the willow.

"Hi! whatcha doin?" "Just playin'," I told him. "Who is that nice lady at your house?" Danny asked.

"Oh, that is Dorothy. She lives with us now." I said it nonchalantly. "My mom told me that is your 'new mommy,' said Danny Boy.

I must have been shocked for, I was speechless, and a cold chill ran down my spine. How could anyone in this world ever try to take the place of my mom? Danny Boy must have known that he'd said something very wrong, because he ran just as fast as his legs could take him out from under my special willow tree.

Walking into the house that summer day, the spring in my step was slower than usual. My cheeks were not as rosy, and I felt a big lump in my throat. I opened the door to the house. "What's wrong, Linda? You look so sad. Can I help?" Dorothy asked.

"No" I said sharply, walking to my room and shutting the door behind me. Curled into a fetal position, I lay on my bed with my doll clutched close to my heart.

"Dolly, what is Danny Boy talking about? Is this true about what he said about Dorothy?"

I refrained from asking Dorothy. Perhaps because I didn't want to know the truth. Days and months passed. I was becoming more belligerent *(she called it rebellious)* every day. Who does this woman think *she is?* She was a good cook, but she wasn't that good!

"Linda, go straighten your room!" Dorothy told me one day. "I don't have to! You can't tell me what to do! *YOU ARE NOT MY MOTHER!"* I ran to my room, jumping in bed and pulling the covers over me. To my surprise, Dorothy followed. "Out of that bed right now!" she said as she pulled the covers back. I was not going to move until I saw the little twig that she held in her hand. *It is small. No way is she going to hit me!* I can't wait to tell Daddy about this.

When I moved off the bed, Dorothy got me right on the leg twice.

"OUCH!" I yelled. *"DON'T TOUCH ME OR I WILL TELL MY DAD!"*

"You go right ahead and tell him," she said firmly. "I have a few things to tell him too.

What did she mean by that? Well, I couldn't wait for Daddy to come home, but I had a big surprise waiting for me.

Dorothy moved around the house easily as she made dinner. It was time for my father to come walking through the door. I was so anxious because every night I got a new toy that he brought home for me. Besides, I wanted to tell him how Dorothy had treated me. I knew he would be so upset with her! Maybe he would tell my mommy to hurry and come home!

"Hi!" The door swung open, and my father walked in. I ran to his arms, but to my surprise, there was nothing in Daddy's hand. I wondered where my toy was. "Daddy, I have to tell you something about Dorothy!" I said. He walked over and kissed Dorothy on the cheek. "How are my two women?" he said. I was getting more impatient.

"Daddy, listen! Dorothy and I had a fight today!" "Really?" he said, giving Dorothy a little grin.

I could not understand this behavior. He was not bothered in the least that Dorothy and I had any kind of problems.

"Linda, you might not like this, but you are to call Dorothy 'MOTHER' from now on, and you must obey her when she tells you to do something," he said.

I must have shown my shock and disbelief because he squeezed me tight and looked deep into my eyes. "I know this is not easy, but it will be in time."

Gosh! I was speechless. This woman had my father in a trance, and I was not winning this time at all. I looked at Dorothy, and she was standing there with a look of appreciation on her face.

"Mommy better come home soon." Things are getting out of hand.

Many more days of disagreements followed, and every time they were put to rest with a little twig off the tree. Soon, I finally got the hint that I should be calling this woman "Mother," and I did it more willingly as time went on. I didn't know she was my stepmother.

CHAPTER III

A Life Without My Willow

Memories of our old house flooded my mind. I missed Danny Boy and my willow tree. My new mommy and my father had sold their homes and bought one together in a town called Gary, Indiana. As a child, I felt we were moving across the world. It was only about 20 minutes away.

It was a nice house, but it was right next to a very busy street where cars came and went at all hours. A little country store stood adjacent to the house on the corner. The street was too busy, and "mommy" would not let me go to the store alone.

"Mommy, please let me go; I have a nickel for some button candy. Daddy gave it to me!"

"OK," she said. My trips to the store were fun and special, I knew the countries by heart. The candy was stacked neatly behind the big glass windows, and I pressed my nose against the pane. The store owner smiled down at me, handing me an extra piece of bubble gum.

"Here, Linda. Make this last you a day." He knew I would be back tomorrow.

My stepmother was waiting for me at the corner, and she took my hand as we walked across the street. I noticed the big leaves crackling under our feet as we walked. They came in all colors: gold, red, orange, brown, and green. Fall was just around the corner, and it was time to shop for school clothes. I was five years old and getting ready for kindergarten.

"Mommy, what is school like?" I asked.

"It is a place to learn and meet lots of new friends."

Even though I was feeling excited, my stomach had a very odd feeling.

We walked hand in hand across the busy street. It was just down the block, but it was my first day of kindergarten, and my stepmother wanted me to feel comfortable. Walking through the big double doors, I was almost trampled by all the kids in the halls. Dorothy asked for directions to my room, and off we went. Walking through the classroom, we were met by a tall young lady who gave us a warm smile.

"Hello," she said. "I am Mrs. Finnigan. And what's your name?"

"Linda," I said, looking sheepishly at Dorothy. There was a worried look on her face, but she managed to let go of my hand, and Mrs. Finnigan introduced me to the class. I could see this was going to be fun. There was a big slide in my room, with play dollhouses and pretend dishes. I liked school, and I continued to enjoy it every day. The fall of the year was so beautiful, and my new stepmother did her best to make me enjoy my school experience.

"Linda, are you ready?" Dorothy put the tin foil on the layered chocolate cake that she had just baked. We were going to the school carnival, and that cake was for the cakewalk.

"Yes, I am, but where is Daddy?"

"Daddy is working the night-shift, and he won't be going with us."

Walking out the door, a great sadness came over me. I realized that I did not get to see my father as often as I would have liked and that I missed him.

Walking into the large hall, we could hear the music and feel the excitement. There were clowns with balloons, face painters, kids dunking fish in the sand, and I saw so many people that I thought I would get lost.

"Don't let go of my hand, honey."

"OK," I said as we walked to the cake room. Then the music began to play, and everyone began to walk around the circle. "Keep walking," Dorothy said.

As the music stopped, I was the only person standing.

"I won! I won!" I was so excited! I was even more excited when I learned that we won the cake that my stepmother made!

Everyone said that Dorothy was the best cook ever. She made pies, cakes, and cookies. Here, applepies and cobblers would not do those of anyone I knew. Every year, she and my father were in the basement canning apples, peaches, pickles, tomatoes, and corn. Even now, I can hear the pressure cookers whistling! Dorothy and Daddy had their own special time, and I felt Daddy had forgotten all about me. This made me very sad.

"Sam, hand me that jar; I need to wash it." "Comin' right up!" my father would say.

I was the best-fed five-year-old around and getting fatter every day. I felt just fine, but already kids were starting to call me names, and I didn't want to go to school.

Sitting at the table on that day, Dorothy had that look in her eye. "Linda, we need to talk."

"What about?"

"About how much you weigh. It is not good for you, and I am going to put you on a diet!"

At that point, I had no idea what a diet was or what I was in for. The next two months were the most miserable ones of my life, and I had no idea that it would be the beginning of what I had to do for the rest of my life. Lunch consisted of a hotdog in tomato soup. I was so hungry that I remember licking my plate when no one was watching me.

"Is that all I get for lunch?" I would ask.

"That's all," Dorothy said. "Now don't complain and just eat it."

It seemed to me that she was being a little too selfish with the portions I was getting. I wasn't very happy until one day, about four weeks later.

"Linda!" my teacher said. "Come here for show and tell. We all want to hear about your diet!"

As I stood in front of the class, I heard the sounds of "ouuuuuuuuu and aaahhhhhhhhh." It was now very noticeable that I had lost fifteen pounds, and I was so proud. As I began to speak, I noticed a boy in the back of the room stretching to see me. Glen Jenkins was his name, and he was the cutest boy I ever saw (next to Danny Boy, that is).

"Mommy! Mommy! I've got a secret! I can't tell you!"

I sang the words over and over. It was my first love, and I just knew I could not tell a soul!

"Linda, what is your secret? I won't tell!" "Oh, it's nothing," I said. I just could not tell anyone about those strange stirrings I felt. It was the first fluttering I had ever felt in my heart. I doubt that Glen Jenkins even remembers who I am. But it doesn't matter. It was a wonderful feeling! How special for a six-year-old!

Three years had passed, and calling Dorothy "mother" became much easier. She was the one who took care of me most every day. We spent many hours together.

The spare bedroom where Dorothy often sat was full of cloth and remnants. She spent many hours sitting in front of the sewing machine, making my clothes and many of hers.

"Linda, how would you like to sew?" she asked one day. "I would love it!"

At eight years old, I was sitting at the machine, learning how to make aprons and potholders.

It was special because that was the time that I spent talking over my daily events at school. There were always stories about "the good old days" when Dorothy was a child. She was a kid in the Depression days when her mom made dresses out of flour sacks.

"What did they look like? Were they white and wrinkled?" I asked.

"No, they were sometimes pretty with different patterns. We were just glad to get anything to wear."

Those stories were sometimes hard for me to hear. I felt sorry for her. Her life had not been an easy one. Sometimes, her siblings would sleep eight in a bed. They would all cuddle up just to keep warm! And then there were babies that died at birth and a sister who passed away at sixteen years of age.

I can remember visiting the home of Dorothy's parents, Grandpa and Grandma Harding. It was a great, big farmhouse on a hill. It seemed like there were all kinds of fascinating nooks and crannies, and we had to go to the outhouse to use the bathroom.

Grandpa would get up every morning to milk the cows and feed the pigs. The big red barn sat behind the house, and the water pump was one hundred yards in front of the barn. Walking to the barn, there was a strong smell of fresh hay mixed with cow manure. I always dread that walk. As I went closer, I felt my stomach do somersaults. The smell was more than I could take.

Grandpa Harding was always working, and Grandma Harding was never out of the kitchen. Her kitchen was filled with heaping bowls of freshly cold milk sitting in the refrigerator, and the heavenly smell of fresh baked biscuits always floated in the air. I loved the farm, but my only problem was sleeping at night.

"Linda, go to sleep!" my mother would say. "I can't," was my reply.

I always slept on the couch in the living room by the big door. It always stood open, and I felt like any minute a big, burly boogieman would run in and snatch me up. I would cover my head and say my prayers until I fell asleep. At dawn, I could hear stirrings in the kitchen. It was still dark, but Grandpa was up and ready to milk the cows.

I was not as close to my step-grandfather and grandmother, but I cherish my childhood memories of the big farm and house on the hill.

My mind carries no memories of the next four years. It is as if an ink bottle spilled on those years, blotting out the memories of shared intimate moments with my beloved mother. I have not been told of her death, and there is an empty place in my heart. What could I have missed in those years? Have I chosen to forget those lonely days or years without the closeness that only a mother could provide? I was a very lonely child, longing for something that would never return.

Dorothy had two sons from another marriage. I thought that was special because now I had two stepbrothers. They were years older than I was, and our relationship was not close because of distance. I was the only child being raised in our home. I saw my sister on occasion, but not as much as I wanted to. She was making her own way in the world and struggling to survive on her own. I know the loss of our biological mother was taking its toll on her life.

Dorothy made the holidays in our house special. They were happy ones, and our house was full of people, with Dorothy making everyone feel comfortable.

Our guests loved Dorothy's cooking, and we all looked forward to dinner time together.

The loss of a parent is one of the most devastating events in a child's life.

> A child reacts differently from an adult when a parent dies. Preschool children see death as temporary and reversible. However, children between five and nine begin to think more like adults about death. The shock of a family member dying may inhibit other family members from dealing with the child's grief. Long-term denial of the death or avoidance of grief can be emotionally unhealthy and can later lead to more severe problems.
>
> (The Counseling Corner, 2001, p.3).

Children who are having serious problems with grief and loss may display one or more of these.

- Loss of appetite
- Reclusiveness
- Inability to sleep
- Depression
- Loss of interest in events and daily activities.
- Withdrawal from friends and family members
- Encopresis

Do not feel that professional help is not needed if these signs are displayed. Trained clinicians, therapists, clinical social workers, and child psychologists are best at helping children deal with grief and loss. Professional help may be the answer for the grieving family to cope with their loss while the professionals are giving assistance to the child's grief or loss.

CHAPTER IV

Come Out from Among Them

One day, while walking in the door from school, I noticed that something was different about the house. It was quiet and somewhat dark. In one of the bedrooms, I could hear a small voice. My mother is weeping.

Her bedroom door was shut, but I could hear her voice speaking. I knew no one was in the house, so I listened quietly. My mother was doing something that was strange to me. She was praying in a language that was unfamiliar. I became frightened but remained silent about the incident.

At dinner that night, my mother announced that attending church was now going to be a regular occasion for us. Well, for my mother and me, anyway. My father was not as enthusiastic about this announcement.

"Just where will you be going?" he asked. I noticed he said "you" and not "we."

My mother chose a Pentecostal church not far from our home, and church became the main focus of our lives. Religion was unknown to me at such a young age, but memories of sleeping on church benches still remain. The next few years of my life are about to be affected by this drastic change in our lifestyles.

"Gunsmoke", "Amos and Andy", "Davy Crockett," and "Howdy Doody" were my favorite television programs. I looked forward to them after school every day. Walking into the house on a warm spring day, I remember setting my books on the table, ready to do my homework. I cannot say that I enjoyed that as much as television. Suddenly, I noticed an empty corner that the television set had previously occupied.

Mom must have moved the living room furniture around. As I searched the room, I found no television at all.

"Hi Linda," Mom said. "How was school?"

"Forget school; where is the TV?" "Ohhhh that!" she said, very nonchalantly.

"We sold it because our preacher said it was not good for our family."

In my ten-year-old mind, I could not begin to imagine what was wrong with "Gunsmoke", "Amos and Andy," "Davy Crockett" or "Howdy Doody". I was upset and felt that someone was depriving me of something I enjoyed very much.

As my mother began to set the stage for what a "Christian home" was supposed to be like, I began to follow her path, not realizing the effect or affect this path would have on the most valuable years of my life. There was the dance class I could not attend because dancing was against my religion. I was the only girl wearing culottes during gym class because wearing shorts and showing your legs were sins. There was no make-up or jewelry. I was not allowed to go to movies, football games, or mixed bathing (swimming with boys and girls together). Wearing pants signified being a man; therefore, women could not wear pants. And a woman's hair was her glory, so putting the scissors to it was definitely out.

"Come out from among them and be separate." Mother would say. At this point, I asked myself, What *could* I do? There was only one thing left. *GO TO CHURCH*!"

It was my tenth birthday, and my mother was preparing for my annual birthday celebration. Birthdays were always special in our home. My tenth year was the most memorable, as it was the year I learned to play accordion, blossomed into adolescence, and learned that my real mother would never return from the place called "Heaven."

Bright-colored balloons hung from the ceiling with streamers. There were party hats, horns, and a big cake sitting in the middle of the table. I was so proud and felt very special. Many of my friends were not given parties such as this, so I always told them that this was their party, too. "Pin the Tail on the Donkey" was a tradition for every party, and we ended with musical chairs. My yearly birthday party was a special gift that my stepmother gave me. It always made me feel special and loved. My last party was given at age nineteen. It was the year I left home.

Summertime was fun and filled with imaginary play. Blocks of wood that were left from the shavings my dad used to build with were my favorite playthings. Waking up in the morning, I would run to the basement, where I had set up a small house that I had made from blocks. Several catalogs sat nearby that I used to cut out people and things that would occupy the house. It was so convenient. The "paper people" could have anything they wanted. All I had to do was cut it from the catalog.

This playtime is something that kept me busy for months during the summer while I waited for school to start in the fall. I was an only child, and this could be a very lonely life. Since I was around adults most of the time, I found myself acting older than I really was. When I was ten years old, I looked thirteen. When I got to be thirteen, I looked eighteen. I thought there something was very strange about this.

Every Saturday, my eyes peaked over the covers as my mother came bursting into my room. "Up! Up! Up!" she said.

Saturdays at our home were housework days, meaning it was cleaning and hair-washing day. The problem is that this was my only day of rest. Wiping the sleep out of my eyes, I struggled to wake up and dress for the daily chores.

"Linda, hurry up now; your oatmeal is on the kitchen table."

The smell of oatmeal and coffee filled the house, along with the peach cobbler that my mother was preparing for our Sunday dinner. My chores consisted of cleaning my room, our family bathroom, and sweeping and dusting the living room. I really did not mind; in fact, I liked it.

Isn't this what women are for? Clean, cook, and keep the man of the house happy. I was being prepared for my future as a woman in this world. *Or was I?*

Many weekends, Daddy would leave quite early in the morning, taking his gun for hunting. He shot ducks, geese, rabbits, squirrels, quail, deer, and the occasional fish. All of his guns hung neatly in a gun rack, where he polished them often. I spent many hours watching him clean the wild game he brought home. I think he missed having a son to hunt, with and he enjoyed our time together during this event.

It was as if he had a system for this cleaning routine. The rabbit's feet would hang from the back of the stairs, where he had nailed each one. Their bodies and legs extended downward, hanging limp.

Daddy's knife would slit from the throat to the end of the belly. I could not watch this part because all the insides would come splattering on the paper that lay beneath the animal. I would uncover my eyes and then run as fast as I could because the smell was more than I could bear.

"It's ok, Linda; the rabbit doesn't know the difference," Daddy would say.

The next night, there would be friend rabbit on my plate. Sometimes the meat was tough, and I found it difficult to eat, but I learned that if I did not eat it, I would surely be hungry. Daddy went hunting often, and when he did, what he bagged would be on the dinner table the next night.

Daddy worked in the steel mills in Gary, Indiana. Shift work was hard, and I can remember how tired he would be when he got home from work. One special thing that I remember most was how my stepmother would get up every day at 5:00 a.m. to make his breakfast and lunch for work. I knew this was a labor of love.

Dorothy and Dad were inseparable. The summers were filled with bushels of corn, apples, peaches, tomatoes, and pickles ready to be canned. Returning home from school on warm days, with the wonderful smells that came from the basement where Mom and Dad slaved over a hot oven with pressure cookers whistling, made my mouth water with anticipation. There was a special room that Dad had made especially for those beautiful jars. Mom would proudly present them at family gatherings and social events at church, where you could hear "oooohhhhhhhh's" and "ahhhhhhhhsssssss" as they were being sampled. "These were Daddy and Dorothy's days to spend time together. I was not a part of this, except for the occasional "popping" of the beans, which consisted of breaking the long beans into different sections. We would have races to see who could do the most in a short time. That was fun and a delightful way to pass the time.

One beautiful Saturday morning, Daddy was putting fresh flowers in the car as if he were preparing to go somewhere. Dorothy said, "Get your coat; we are going to the graveyard." I really didn't know what a graveyard was. As we drove up, I saw all the beautiful flowers lined up in rows. Daddy parked the car in front of a grave that did not have flowers. At the foot of the big grave lay a tiny grave.

"Why don't you take Linda for a walk?" Daddy said to his mother. There was a look of disapproval on her face.

Strolling along the riverbank, Dorothy and I made small talk, mostly about the pretty flowers. I had no idea my father was putting flowers on my mother's and the baby's graves.

After returning home from the graveyard, we spent the rest of Saturday getting ready for church. Mom always plopped me on the kitchen cabinet to wash my long hair. As I was lying on my back, she would pour cupfuls of water from the sink through my hair. This was our time for small talk, and it was business as usual. Our conversation began about my days as a little girl, and I began asking questions about my biological mother. To this day, I will never know how anyone thought I knew of my mother's death. I could have denied the fact that she was gone forever. But no one had explained what death really was.

"Why Linda! Don't you know that your mother is no longer alive?" At that moment, someone took a hammer to the pit of my stomach. I wanted to run, scream, and cry. I wanted my mother. Knowing that she would never return was one of the most devastating events that ever happened to me. In my dark room that night, I wept in silence for a mother I would never have. Everyone else was over this event that happened long ago. For me, it was only the beginning. I have mourned the loss of my mother since the day I was told she had gone to a place called "heaven." That was 3 years ago.

I didn't know if I would ever understand this traumatic event. I only knew that a great void had taken me to a place in my life, and I wanted it filled with love, compassion, and understanding.

Feeding children excessive food to help them forget their grief and loss will lead to adult obesity, heart disease, and possibly death.

According to Jamie Ackerman Foster, MPH, RD, LD, of Case Western University, "30.3% of children ages 6 through 11 years of age are overweight, and 15% are obese. Researchers have identified many risk factors. Genetic and common eating habits are both likely causes" pg.1

It is important for children to learn healthy eating habits. It is suggested that diets for children at a young age could lead to eating disorders. In (Newman and Newman 1999, (p. 317) states that a child who eats excessively feels inferior and ashamed. "Individuals who suffer from bulimia are usually ashamed of their eating and often eat in secret".

Children who are obese feel a loss of control, followed by self-criticism and depression. (American Psychiatric Association, 1994).

CHAPTER V

The Wonder Years

I searched for answers. It was difficult for anyone to talk about the event, and it wasn't until later that I understood why everyone would keep this from me.

My mother passed away while she was delivering a baby boy. It seems that she had sclerosis of the liver, which it affected the baby. The story goes, from what I understand, that she passed first, and then a doctor asked my father if he wanted the baby to have a transfusion. My father declined because he reasoned that he would not be able to care for an infant. He now had my sister and I to think about, and how could he manage a baby too? Years later, he and I had discussions about this. He felt so traumatized that he did not remember what really went on, and so many decisions were made without thinking about them.

These discussions I had with my father were very strained. He had a very difficult time talking about them, but it helped me resolve issues in my own mind about my mother's death.

In my father's closet hung a robe. It was multicolored and silk. I wondered why he never wore it.

It was a gift from my real mother, and Dorothy, an understanding wife, let it remain in the closet.

My father had a collection of ties that would have filled a truck. When we went to church, he looked like he was the preacher himself. He was a handsome man, and when he wore a hat, the brim went over one eye, giving him a gangster look. On many occasions, I told him, as little girls do, that I wanted to grow up and marry him. I had no idea what marriage meant, but I knew that no one measured up to my "daddy."

The days were long, and soon the trees began to shed their leaves. Walking to school, I could hear the brightly colored leaves crackle beneath my feet. I was growing up —a little too fast, I might add.

At the age of ten, bras and periods did not suit me all that much. There were miserable days at school when cramps were unbearable and boys took delight in snapping my bra without a moment's notice. I did not understand why all this had to happen to me, but I took every advantage to look older than I was. I enjoyed having the boy's attention. I was longing to fill the loneliness I felt inside. Sixth grade was the year of pimples, bras, high heels, and sweaters —all the things that made you a young woman —and I was enjoying every minute of it. I was beginning to open my eyes to the opposite sex.

My evening ritual was practicing the accordion. This was something I enjoyed so much, and it was an outlet from the world. I learned so fast, and soon I was taking piano lessons from the nice pastor's wife at our church. She was so sweet, and it seemed as though she could play any musical instrument. Her voice was like that of an angel from heaven. I idolized her, and she was the person who taught me so much about music. Soon, my parents bought me a piano, and I was on my way to being the church pianist.

Church was the center and focus of our family's life. It was difficult being called "freak," "weird," and "ugly". No matter how hard I tried, I never fit in. Some of the girls I hung out with were nice but were always asking me questions about my religion. My hair was so long and unmanageable. It was piled so high on top of my head that I thought I would topple over. I spent my whole lunch hour after swimming class just to making my hair presentable for the next class. I never went to the parties that I was asked to, and I was not allowed to socialize with kids "in the world." The days of "miniskirts" were my worst nightmare. All my skirts and dresses were worn so long that I was laughed at and teased constantly. Surely, I was a freak of nature and was doomed to stay that way. The years that should have been the most wonderful years of my life turned out to be the ones that I lost and will never retrieve.

It was a swelteringly hot summer day. Eighth grade was finally coming to an end. The teacher was calling out everyone's name to get their report cards. I watched with anticipation as every child walked to the front and then back to their desk. I was the only one left. I waited. The class was dismissed. I felt as if the chill of death had fallen upon me. I was the last child sitting in the room, and I could not move. I knew something was very wrong, but I did not know what. I asked the teacher where my report card was. She replied, "Linda, you will have to go and speak to the principal."

Tears filled my eyes as I walked to the principal's office. "Linda," he said, I am sorry. You were the only one we questioned. We called your mother, and she told us to fail you." I felt weak, and my heart started to pound. At this moment, I felt the same exact loss that I felt upon learning of my real mother's death. I walked home that day with great sorrow. I could not go on to be with my other friends in high school. I was not only a freak, but now I was stupid. Everyone would know, and I would be shamed. Walking up to the house, I felt rage and hate for a woman who called herself my mother. Opening the door, I remembered the look on her face. It was one of disdain. I bore my pain in silence because I had no voice. Children were to be seen and not heard.

To this day, I do not understand how anyone would think I could possibly do my homework and go to church every single night for weeks upon weeks during revivals. Education was not promoted in my home. It was more important to go to church and live for God. The oppression that I felt as a child foreshadowed events that followed me in sequence throughout my life. Could anyone not see that this was too much for a child to handle? Only one person did. And that was my grandpa.

"Linda, that is an awful lot of religion for such a little girl," he said one day as we swung on the porch swing.

"Aw, Grandpa, you know how it is." He loved me and wanted only what was best for me, but no one knew how it really was except me. The family that I knew and loved was now so far away because "they" were not Christians and there was no common ground with "our" family.

Decisions made by parents have consequences for their children as adults. Some of the things we know about self-esteem are:

- Children begin forming beliefs about themselves early in life.
- Children look to parents and other important adults for evidence that they're lovable, smart, and capable.
- Self-esteem affects school success.
- Self-esteem affects how children relate to other people. Self-esteem affects creativity.
- Parents affect their children's self-esteem.

What Parents Can Do:

- Praise your children.
- Show your children lots of love and affection. Treat your children with respect.
- Be consistent.
- Don't demand perfection from your children.
- Pay attention to your behavior and attitudes. Listen to and respond to your children.
- Keep the promises you make to your children.
- Spend time with your children.
- Teach your children to use positive self-talk.
- Encourage your children to make some decisions for themselves.
- Give your children some responsibility.
- Give your children the freedom to take risks.
- Encourage your children's friendships.
- Encourage your children's interests and abilities.

CHAPTER VI

My First Love

I played the accordion in church often. It was fun, and I began to realize that I could do something after all. Later, I began to take piano lessons, playing by note. I remember clearly that on one occasion, the teacher played a song and told me to "try" to play it. I played it back to her without the book, and she was so upset that she refused to give me any more lessons. My ear was running away with me!

In my music, I excelled far beyond what I imagined. Playing for choirs, for weddings, and for special occasions has been a wonderful experience. My music has been there for me in the darkest hours of despair, and it has never left me. Surely, this was a gift from God. As I began to play for many different functions, I began to feel better about myself, and my self-esteem started to return. I was a star at church camps and places where I could lend my talent. I looked up to. The younger kids in church would often tell me, "I want to be just like you when I grow up." That always made me feel good, but still, I had this undeniable tugging at my heart.

Lying awake at night, I would watch the busy cars with their bright lights. Sometimes it was difficult to sleep. Who was I, and what would I make of my life? Church had become the focus of my life, and many of my extracurricular activities were built around it. Becoming a teenager was fun as long as I obeyed the rules of the church. The teenage group at church was all friends. We have many memories of our youth. There were ice cream socials and Sunday afternoons at church spent jamming together with our instruments and singing. We had picnics, hayrides, and ice-skating parties. We were a very close-knit group that stuck together no matter what. There was the occasional tiff, but we would just work it out. To this day, many of us are still connected.

Thirteen was a very interesting year. Suddenly, it happened on a Sunday night —my first encounter with love. I was engrossed in my piano playing at church that night. My fingers were flying over the keyboard, and I kept looking at the organist to see if she thought I was keeping up. As I looked in her direction, my eyes turned to the left, where they met the guitarist. That was it! I had been smitten by the love bug!

His name was Tommy, and I was in a trance. Of course, he didn't know I was alive, but it didn't matter. I took every opportunity I could to look at him or be where he was, and there were times when I "thought" I had a chance. After all, we both played music! Well, that was until he ended up getting engaged. I can remember crying as I sat and watched him walk down the aisle with his new bride. I knew I had lost him to another woman. I could never love another. After all, I was thirteen, and time was running out!

I was getting used to the fact that I would be repeating the eighth grade over and over. I had just gotten a job at an ice cream shop and was preoccupied by other things. I was friendly and somewhat outgoing, but there was still a void in my life. I would confide in my friends, and they couldn't understand why I was unhappy and told me it was just a phase. Maybe they were right. But something still seemed very wrong to me. It is now clear to me what was going on. I just did not know what it meant.

It was Monday evening. I walked in the door and was greeted with a hug and a kiss from my father. One thing is for sure: there was plenty of love in my family. Lots of affection and expressions of love. I said hello to Mom, and the dinner table was set. We always ate when dad got home around 3:30 or 4:00 p.m. We sat down to eat and chatted about the usual events of the day. How is school? How was work?

After dinner, I felt like I might have eaten too much and was a little queasy. Walking into the bathroom that night, I shut the door, bent over the toilet, and automatically threw up. No finger down the throat. Just by bending over, I could do this. I felt better and somewhat relieved. I was in control of something.

I had never heard of the eating disorder bulimia. This was a ritual that I had every night for the next 12 years of my life. I was the "perfect child"! How could this be? Who could I turn to? Where could I go? I had been taught to depend on God. So, I prayed every night, and I knew he heard my prayer. Now I lay me down to sleep. I pray to the Lord for my soul to keep. If I should die before I wake, I pray to the Lord for my soul to take. God bless Mommy, Daddy, and the whole world. Help me and make everything OK. Amen. I repeated this prayer each night. It stuck with me into my adult life and was my source of strength —that my unseen protector was with me all the time.

Little things seemed to unravel, one step at a time. It wasn't that our family was private, but I just didn't pay attention to things. One day, my father and mother were talking about this person named "Jimmy". When the discussion was all over, I found out that I had a half-brother that my father had not seen since he was four years old. This amazed me, as I couldn't understand how it could be. My mother suggested that we look him up and see where he was. When my father found him, we planned a trip to Kansas to meet him. I wondered how this would affect their relationship after all these years. I was very excited about the fact that I had an older brother and was about to meet him for the first time.

We arrived in Kansas early in the morning, and I noticed that my father was a little nervous. I guess I was, too, but I was so anxious that I didn't let it show. I was sixteen, and above all else, I wanted to make a good impression. At least my hair wasn't piled on my head anymore, and I did look pretty good for my age. Self-confidence was taking over.

We walked up to the door, and I got the biggest surprise of my life. I found myself staring into the eyes of a man who could have been my twin. There was no doubt; I had a brother, and he was my father's son. We all looked just alike. We shook hands and made the formal introductions. My brother Jimmy was thirty years old. This was the beginning of a wonderful relationship in our family.

My life seemed pretty ordinary to me, with the exception of a few things: bulimia, loneliness, and low self-esteem. I felt as though my nightly rituals were strange, but I tried to act as normal as possible. I was frustrated with school. Shuffling my life between church, school, and homework was very difficult. There was no time, and all my energy was directed toward church. I learned to believe that church was the only thing I had in my life, although there really were lots of things going on.

The church that I attended was having severe problems. It was on the verge of a split. People were not getting along, and there was talk in our house about looking around for another "church home". All of this made me feel very insecure. Church was my life, and it seemed that everything was falling apart.

I continued to look for serenity and self-acceptance among all of this chaos. There was a lot of love present, but there was also an undercurrent of, "It's never good enough." Whatever I did, there was always room for improvement. I had a hard time defining my own self. Living a double life had become as normal as everyday living. On my way to school, I stopped at my friend Nancy's house and changed my clothes, my hairdo, and put on make-up. I must have looked okay, I thought. At least no one laughed or made fun of me anymore, and that was a relief. I felt more like a human being. I knew my parents would be upset if they knew, but it didn't matter. I just wanted to find happiness and a life where I could be happy with myself.

I thought I found this in my first "real" boyfriend. He was handsome, smart, and a Christian. Things that happened in this relationship were dysfunctional, but I didn't know the difference because of my age. Latching on to him for dear life before knowing what a normal relationship should be was detrimental to my life and my youthful development. I dated him throughout my teenage years and married him almost on the day of my graduation. My two children, Cara and Phillip, were with him, and we later divorced. I was young, I was hurt, and I needed love, compassion, and healing that could only come from above.

The Meaning of Love

Love comes in many different forms. Dr. Andrew Newbery, Wiktionary Encyclopedia, suggested that physical love is similar to that of drugs because, without it, humanity would die out. A crush or infatuation is characterized by intrusive thinking (Dorothy Tennov, August 29, 1928 to February 3, 2007). These are obsessive thoughts or feelings about a specific person.

At the age of 13, a teenager does not know the true meaning of love but feels infatuation or a crush. True love comes through knowing and accepting a person for who they are. This "crush" is something experienced by every person who experiences infatuation for the first time.

CHAPTER VII

A Life of Searching

During this marriage, I had a very special friend named Becky. Without her and her many hours of selfless giving, I would have been very miserable. We would sit and talk for hours on end at the kitchen table. Our favorite snack was iced tea, bratwurst, and crackers. We were well acquainted with Weight Watcher diets and having babies. We sewed, shopped, baked, and talked every day on the phone. I named my second daughter after her and pray that she knows how special she was in my life.

I was twenty-four with my second child and on my way to Europe with my first husband. I spent 3 years there with my first husband as he worked with the Europeans and the American military. We were missionaries and lived in a town named Kaiserslautern, Germany. These were years of growing and gaining independence in my life.

Often, we took trips to other places for church meetings and events.

Europe was beautiful. Waking up, I bounced out of my feather bed in a bed and breakfast in Holland. Looking out the window, my eyes were almost blinded by the beauty of the red tulips surrounding the big windmill. How lucky I am. I will never forget this beautiful sight. Just then, my breakfast was delivered on a white wicker tray with a shiny white plate holding fresh fruit and a German bread called *brochen*. A tiny rose in a small vase was placed perfectly on the corner of the tray. Why must I leave this beauty? Returning to Kaiserslautern, I began the ritual of going to church meetings and helping other members of the church. It was just about time for the birth of my second child, so I busied myself while waiting for this wonderful experience.

My son was born in a German hospital. It was about 3:00 p.m. Dr. Hans Linden walked into the room and told me that he would soon give me an injection. I had been miserable and called him every day. He decided to just start my labor. All through the previous night, nuns came to my room bearing white pots and broches with butter. They were so friendly, and the tea was just what I needed for the long night ahead. At two in the morning, two nuns entered my room, and speaking German, told me to put on my robe. We were going to the delivery room.

Why are we going there, and I am not even in labor?

Soon I was put in a tub of warm water that went to my neck. The water was warm, and I felt weightless. They took me out of the tub, and I was told to "touch my toes." As I did this, they took out a metal syringe. They were going to give me the enema ritual that I remembered so long ago.

At that moment, I stood up and spoke very harshly, "NEIN." I said, which means no in German.

They were very unhappy with me, but I really did not care. I was placed on a gurney and wheeled to a room where ten other women lay. When they placed me, I looked over and saw other women having their babies one after another. This was so different from what I had experienced with my firstborn, Cara, in the United States. I looked up and saw my physician, Hans Linden. Relief crossed my face because he reassured me that I was OK. It was beyond me how I would have this baby if I were not in labor yet.

As women began to have their babies and the placenta was delivered, nurses would have them get up and walk to the other side of this same delivery room to their hospital bed. This truly amazed me. German women are known for their strength, and they were sure proving it to me on that day.

"Dr. Hans, I won't be able to walk to the other side of the room after I have this baby," I said.

I wanted to let him know that I was not German and that this is not done in the United States. He again assured me that I would be "just fine."

About ten minutes later, a woman stepped to the foot of my bed, my feet were put in stirrups, and another woman standing at my head lifted me up and told me to push.

"I am not in labor!" I protested.

Labor or not, I was out like a light. I was not aware of my baby's birth until I woke up several minutes later. "Ok, now you will go to that bed on the other side of the room," Dr. Linden said. I knew they were in for a surprise because I was much too weak to get up off my bed and walk after the birth of my child.

Helping me sit up, they pulled me to stand. I saw the bed, and it looked like a mile away to me. I felt weak, and as they let go, I moved my foot to walk and collapsed. Lying on the floor, they peered down at me like I was a sick weakling. A wheelchair was summoned, and the nurse wheeled me to my bed. Lying there, I wondered if I had a boy or a girl. Soon, one of the nuns came in carrying a child who had been swaddled in a tight blanket. I asked her if it was Herr or Daemon. "Shurn Herr," she replied. I had a beautiful baby boy. James Hans Phillip was his name.

My days in the hospital were long, and I began to get weary. I was assured that my son was being fussed over in the nursery. He was the only American who had been born in the hospital at Landstuhl. I returned home to Haus Bethel. The nights were cold and long, and I was torn between my love for my children and the absence of a man who was never with me in body or mind.

My marriage was now in shambles, and I had nowhere to turn except my parents. I flew to their home in Bloomington, Indiana. They took me in and tried their best to help, but it was no use. I was unhappy and turned everywhere I could to find love and happiness.

Six months later, I found myself in a second marriage. I had hope for this marriage, and from it came two beautiful girls, Rebecca and Elena. This marriage also did not last. My search for happiness, I learned, was not to be found in men. The problem was that it took some people longer than others to learn.

As a *"woman of God,"* I began to pray and ask for direction in my life. How could I get anywhere if I kept changing men and where I lived? The only security that I had and knew I would always have were my children. They were everything to me.

So, I began my life on my own. Settling in an apartment in Salinas, California, I looked to the system for help in my time of need. My parents helped me buy a car, and I began to look for a job. Attending Hartnell College in Salinas, California, part-time put me on my way to a nursing degree. The first job I landed was in a hospital as a certified nursing assistant. This was wonderful, for it offered me a way out of the system and a start to recovering my self-worth. I was well liked at the hospital and enjoyed my work. I went from working on the floor to working in surgery. It was enjoyable getting to know the doctors and learning the surgery ward "lingo." Surely, I was coming up in the world, until one day the head nurse called me into her office.

"Linda, there have been some complaints from the other nurses. You seem to be mixing up the surgery sets, and they have not been documented correctly."

This surprised me because I had been careful to do everything just right. In surgery one day, I asked one of the doctors if he had heard anything. It seemed the word was out that I was well liked, and some did not like that. There is one thing I have learned: wherever you go, you do not have to do anything to not be liked. Women can make your life miserable. And that is just what they did.

Reporting to work one day, I walked in, and the head nurse told me, "Sorry, Linda, there is nothing to do today."

I found that quite strange until I realized what was really going on. I was being quietly squeezed out. I took this in stride, knowing that I had children to care for. I walked into another hospital on the other side of town, and I had a job the next week. I was having problems working hospital hours with small children. I was taking sick time when they were sick, and I was working when I was sick.

CHAPTER VIII

Over to the Other Side

When I walked into the emergency room of Salinas Valley Memorial, a familiar voice said, "Hi, Linda, how are you?"

"Oh, I could be better," I replied.

"Why don't you come over to the office and put in an application?" He told me.

It was one of the orthopedic doctors I knew, and I said to myself, Just maybe I should do it. I took a chance and decided to check it out. Of course, I got the job, but the pay was not that good. They decided to start me higher than some of the other girls. I assured the office manager that it would be a secret. That is, until one of the other office girls saw my check on the doctor's desk. What a nightmare!

That was when it all started. I call it the "Linda hate club." No one would speak to me. I was like the misfit in the office. There were at least ten girls working at one time, and I even got a job for one of my best friends. I had worked there for 3 years, and she was not speaking to me either. Of course, she couldn't be my friend, or she would lose her job! Now, the queen bee (who was the office manager) was just as bad. She would call me in the office and say, "Do you know what the girls in the office are saying about you?"

It was my fourth year at the office, and I was beginning to know the meaning of the word "hate". By this time, I knew it was time to leave. When

I left, I don't remember saying "goodbye," but I do remember that a pattern of job to job was forming in my life, and I was getting so tired!

Lord, help me! I need a job, or my kids will suffer! It was 1986, and my two oldest children were living with their father in Cleveland. This helped, but my heart wanted them with me so much that I did not sleep well, and it was affecting my quality of life. One day the phone rang, and it was Phillip. By this time, he was eleven.

"Hi Phillip, how are you?"

There was silence on the other end. "Phillip, talk to me. What is wrong?"

He began to cry. "Mom, I miss you, and I am so unhappy." I am at a phone booth, and I just ran away."

This is a mother's worst nightmare, especially when you are so far away and can do nothing. "Phillip, get yourself back home this minute! If you don't, I will call your father."

"Mom, can I come back home? I miss you."

My conversation with him made me take another look at our lives. We made arrangements, and he came back to live with me. Shortly after that, Cara came too. My apartment was much too small to accommodate four children and myself, so we moved to a small house in town. At the time, my father was very sick, and I began to think of the possibility of moving back east to help my stepmother care for him. This would be difficult with the children, and I had to really think constructively about this. I was very close to my father, and being away during this time of his life would be difficult.

Looking for another job became a hassle. Rebecca and Elena were not happy with their school, and I began to get notes from their teachers requesting parent-teacher conferences. My son, Phil, was a happy boy. He had lots of friends, and he was into surfing. Always good at sports, he hung out with a group of kids like himself. Cara worked as an assistant manager at an apartment complex and was very happy. I felt like life was finally coming together.

I received a call one day regarding a job at Primus Clinic, a brand-new military clinic in the area. Juggling my personal life with my kids and career become challenging. I felt like I had to leave, but I also felt bad about it. "Linda, just do it!" my friend Lynn said. We won't be young forever, you know." Lynn was so cute. She was older but very youthful, and she had her pick of the younger men. "Oh, Lynn, I don't know. Maybe I am not ready yet." "There is no such thing as ready. You just have to dive in!"

She decided to get me diving.

"I will pick you up at 7:00 p.m. sharp." Where are we going?" I asked.

"I don't know. We will see. Somewhere fun!"

I felt strange walking to my car that evening in my shimmering pink blouse. Lynn was a fun girl, but this was not the time for me to be having fun. I had four kids and a job at Primus. Lynn worked there, too. She should know what this is like, as she had two older children. Like two kids, we hauled ourselves down the highway as though we knew where we were going.

The car screeched to a halt.

"We are here," she said, right in front of Fort Ord. I looked around and saw nothing but men in uniform.

"Are we here for dinner?"

"You might say that," she answered.

As we walked in, we heard a few wolf whistles. I guess we look pretty good. Lynn was all smiles, and it was clear that she was going to have a good time. The music was playing loud, and walking into the room, I could hardly see the smoke. I saw the stage out of the corner of my eye. I had heard the women so often talk about these places where some husbands wouldn't allow their wives to go and others couldn't wait to send them. I was a churchgoing girl, and I should not be caught dead at a place like this. I was here, and the lights were beginning to get very dim. I looked at Lynn, and her eyes were as big as saucers!

"Lynn, what is going to happen now?" "Shhhhhhhh, you will see, just wait." I call the next thirty minutes of time I spent there "education personified."

He walked out on stage with his dark blue uniform and black hat. The music began to playing— slow, seductive music. The women were ecstatic, and I was the only one sitting in my chair looking like I was in a church pew. Lynn looked at me. "Why are your hands over your eyes? You just have to see this, hon. Now, look!" And I did.

Lynn and I were like magnets. I think she drew the men, and I kept them there. I was much more reserved. A blonde with green eyes and less flighty than Lynn, I approached life with a much calmer attitude. This made no difference tonight. I was about to get Mr. Cop's hat thrown right in my lap!

Splat! It came flying like a saucer across the stage! Lynn swore he aimed for her. Yeah, I know he did!

What an exhausting night!

"Never again," I told myself. I belong at home with the kids. I never returned to the place I heard everyone call "Sin City."

By this time, I had thrown myself into counseling. I was a wreck. Work was taking a lot out of me. I didn't feel good, but I kept going. The kids had to eat, and now I had all four of them with me. It was a family atmosphere, and I loved having them all around me. So, I could not complain.

The girls and I were close, and most of the time we got along. They had different moods and emotions, and for good measure, there was a boy to break the monotony. His sisters loved Phil, and I could say he was a little spoiled, but he was a good boy, and we all loved him. Our home was filled with lots of love but a little dysfunction too. The children had to contend with my sporadic jobs and our moving around from house to house. I saw the effects of that on all the children and began to slightly worry as I started another new job.

Moving around constantly was certainly different.

I guess that is what all single mothers go through when they are trying to make a living. I was going from house to house, job to job, and man to man. I was getting more and more tired as time passed. Now, starting with my third marriage, I was seriously starting to doubt men in general. "Can't any of them understand?" I thought. I really did not understand what was going on in my life until I began to search for answers. For guidance and direction, I made an appointment with a local therapist.

It was 3:00 a.m. There was a soft knock at the front door. Who could that be at this time of night? It was my daughter, Cara.

As she walked in, I could see she had been crying. "Mom," she said. I went home and found my husband with another woman!"

Oh no! By now she could start reading the book My Mother, Myself. She is starting her life like I did.

"Come in, honey. You can stay here with us."

Cara had been married for a year and was about two months pregnant. She was so fragile and traumatized by this whole event. The next few weeks were spent taking her back and forth to the hospital. I began to think she was going to lose this child.

I stopped at the fabric store on my home from work the next day. I had already planned to start making a quilt for the baby and thought this might help Cara become more involved in the happiness of motherhood. I bought white eyelet and red material with yards and yards of lace for trim. She greeted me with a hug and a kiss.

"Come see what I bought!" I said. She was not expecting this, and I knew she would be "Mom, that is beautiful! Will you help me cut the squares?"

"Of course! We can start right after dinner." This was our next bonding experience as mother and daughter. Cara has been through so much with me, and I love her so much. This was a great experience for me, as this was my first grandchild.

I had, however, begun to have problems with Phillip. My handsome son began to skip school.

"Phil, where did you go?"

"Awwwwwwww mom, the surf's up! You know, I couldn't miss it. I left early and meant to get back in time for school. I was too late."

"Phil, I will have to go to school tomorrow."

Sitting in the office at school, the school counselor looked at me helplessly. "Ms. Madison, I am sorry, but your son needs to understand how important school is."

"My son does know how important school is." I told her. One of the problems everyone has is that he is a good student and makes good grades even though he skips school. I will make sure that he is in school.

But I couldn't. His father and I were in contact occasionally, and I knew if Phil did not graduate, I would be blamed.

My third marriage was a fiasco. It is true that it is difficult to find someone who will love your kids and take them in as their own. Not only that, but sharing a woman with her children is just as difficult. This was my situation. He did not understand and thought that I catered to them. He was jealous and ended up taking his anger out on the children.

I could not have Cara any more traumatized than she already was. He could not understand why I would let her live with us. This was more than I could bear. And next thing I knew, I was out of that marriage. I could not believe it! I truly felt that the devil was out to get me and my family.

Single parenthood is one of the most difficult tasks for a woman. To me, it is one of the most difficult jobs in the world.

A woman must take on both parenting roles: provider, protector, and nurturer. If dealing with a divorce, she will experience grief, anger, guilt, loneliness, and despair. Marilyn Heins, M. D., F.A.A.P. (1989)

- Here are some suggestions that Dr. Heins gives to single mothers:
- Deal with reality. Take care of your needs so you can take care of your children.
- Eliminate unnecessary chores. Save your energy for important matters.
- Spend time apart from the kids to be alone. Exercise. Buy a video.
- Keep a diary of your thoughts, feelings, and progress. Join with other single parents.
- Realize and accept the fact that your children will react to NOT having a father.
- Let your children know your feelings, whether you are sad or happy.
- Involve your children in other families that have children.
- Do not involve your children with people you are dating.
- Don't badmouth the children's father.
- Keep your sense of humor.
- Enjoy your children.

Children thrive in many different kinds of families. Don't waste time worrying about your single life. Embrace it and accept it. Live life to the fullest!

CHAPTER IX

A Memorable Christmas

It was October, and the weather started to get cooler in California. I had just left my job in an orthopedic office to work at a rehabilitation center. My household began to settle down, and the kids seemed to be happy that Thanksgiving and Christmas were just around the corner.

I loved the holidays. As a child, my stepmother always made sure our times were special, and I wanted to do that for my family. Christmas was the greatest time of all. I was leaving the house very early every morning and returning home late at night. I did not worry so much about the children because Cara was there with them. She was beginning to look very maternal, as her baby was due around the first of December.

Walking down the stairs one day, I noticed a ringing in my right ear. Hummm, I wonder if my blood pressure is OK. It was very annoying, but I thought it would go away. I made an appointment to see our family doctor.

"No, Linda you just have tinnitus. Everyone has it once in their life. Just get plenty of rest, and it will go away."

"OK," I said with relief.

Days passed, and I still found myself with this awful ringing. I began to notice a strange metallic taste in my mouth. Oh no, I need to go to the dentist. I must be getting another cavity.

As I sat in the dentist's chair, I explained to him the very strange taste in my mouth. "Linda, this is probably that old cap that is about five years old.

You just need another one. Let's try porcelain this time instead of metal. Of course, it will be a bit more expensive, but it will be worth it."

"Ok," I said, knowing full well that I had no dental insurance. Those were days of doing what you had to do just to make it. That included writing bad checks at the grocery store just so the children could eat.

A few times at work, I noticed my balance seemed off. But this was allergy season, so I just let it go. Work was OK, but I noticed that I was having a difficult time concentrating and working with numbers. This was not good, as I had just started this job and did not remember some of the information I was given. I had been on the job for two weeks when the boss came to me.

"Linda, I am sorry, but we have chosen another candidate for the job. Thank you for your time with us; your check will be ready today before you leave."

I was devastated! I felt faint. I wanted to run, scream, and cry. Doesn't anyone understand? I needed to work! My children needed to eat! This was a hopeless situation. I went home and broke the news to Cara, and the next day we started making plans for me to get unemployment.

Standing in the long unemployment line was my first lesson in humility. I had always been able to provide for the children and myself. I am a good mother. This was just so unusual for me that I couldn't understand why I couldn't get work. I knew I was qualified for many different things. I had been a waitress, clerk, retail supervisor, office manager, and seamstress. I could do so many things, yet no opportunity presented itself. This was one of the lowest times in my life, and I did not know how I was going to fix it, and that was the problem. I couldn't.

The kids were happy, and life went on as usual. Unemployment was not enough to live on, but I did get child support, and that helped me through the next most difficult time of my entire life. I had already been to several doctors, and all they would say was, "You have tinnitus. So many people have it, and it is just a matter of getting used to it."

The high-pitched ringing in my ear really bothered me. It was loud, and it was difficult to concentrate. In my heart, I knew something was wrong, but I did not want to give in. I am a survivor, and having been in the medical field for so long, I usually diagnose my own problems most of the time. Not having much money, I learned a lot of home remedies for helping myself and the children through colds and flu.

It was December 1990, and everyone was getting ready for Christmas. Taking the kids shopping for Christmas was a little more difficult this year. I had started to feel sick, and my head would sometimes swim as I walked around. This worried me, but I did not say anything to the children. I really did not want them to worry unnecessarily. Sitting at the church Christmas play, I enjoyed all the music and scenes. But as I got up to leave, everything turned black. I wondered if I was going to pass out. I felt conscious and let it pass. Now I knew I had something to worry about.

"Hey, Mom." Cara said one day. She was reading the TV Guide, something she never did. "Here is a doctor who does ear tests.

"Look! It is for ringing in the ear. The first one is free with this coupon."

I looked at it and thought, I better go and see what is wrong with my ear. The noise was so loud that I had a difficult time hearing. I felt uncomfortable about going, but I realized it was better to know than not to know.

It was Tuesday, and I could see the relief on Cara's face as I got dressed to go to the doctor. I really couldn't wait to get some medication to take care of this. Finally, I would find a doctor who could help me.

Sitting in the comfortable chair, the doctor looked concerned. With every beep he made, I raised my hand. I could see the strange, disapproving look on his face as he repeated certain sounds. Looking straight at me, he said, "Linda, I don't mean to scare you, but you have no hearing in your right ear. We have to be concerned about these types of things, so I am sending you to an ear, eyes, nose and throat doctor."

"Ok," I said. This really is starting to sound strange. He picked up the phone and made the call that same day.

I knew this was not the norm in the medical field, unless there was a problem. Fear gripped my heart, and I prayed, "Lord, please let everything be OK. If it isn't, give me the strength to go through this." It was probably not until this moment that I became aware of how much my faith and spirituality meant to me.

In the ear doctor's office, he did the necessary hearing test that the other doctor had already performed. Covering all their bases. But I noticed that he kept doing one particular test over and over again. Why can't he just get it right? The look of concern he wore as he did these tests worried me.

"Linda, don't worry. We are going to find out what it is that is bothering you. I am going to set up an MRI for you as soon as possible."

Now, I have been in medicine for enough years to know that when they can't see something they are looking for, you are "bound for the tube."

Driving home that evening, it was cold, and I was feeling very lonely, wondering why this was happening to me. The MRI was set up for the next week. I fretted because I was claustrophobic and afraid to get an MRI. I think I was more concerned about the MRI itself than whether I had a problem.

Everything was on edge. The children were quieter than usual. It was all I could do to keep from becoming withdrawn and consumed with myself. Rebecca was 12, Elena was 10, Phillip was 16, Cara was 20 and she was expecting her first child. These were tough ages to be having difficulties in a home. I moved around the house systematically, trying not to show a lot of concern. I wanted to be strong for them. Knowing the importance of being strong in a man's world. I had no education, and I was a single mom. They all knew I was worried, and, by chance, my third husband came around during this time.

him.

"Hey! Would you like to go with me to my MRI?" I asked

"Sure," he said. I dreaded that day so much that I was willing to go with anyone to that horrible room.

When I entered the trailer, I saw one of the doctors I knew from the hospital sitting at the imaging screen.

"Hi! how are you?" I asked him. We made small talk, but I was very nervous. I looked inside and saw the big MRI. It was a gigantic tube-shaped instrument. Actually, it did not look as bad as I originally thought.

As I was slowly moved into the tube, I began to think about the things in life that really mattered to me. This consisted of three things: my life, my children, and my spirituality. That is when it began. A renewed vow for my commitment to him. The Lord is my shepherd; I shall not want. He makes me lie down in green pastures; He leads me beside the still waters; He restores my soul. Yea, tho I walk through the valley in the shadow of death, I will fear no evil: for thou art with me; thy rod and thy staff comfort me…"

"I knew I was repeating the Twenty-Third Psalm for a specific reason, and I kept repeating, I am doing this for my children.

It was a relief when I was out of that awful tube, but meeting the doctor's gaze in the next room was worse. Not many people know this look. But the medical field had taught me well. With a shake of the hand and that look in his eye, he said,

"Linda, good luck." It was all in the way he said it. Walking out of there that day, I knew it was only a matter of time.

I was right. Arriving home, I felt weak and nervous. The phone rang within an hour.

"Linda, come back to my office right away; I want to show you the results of the MRI," he said forcefully. I grabbed my coat and headed for the car, not wanting any questions asked. I didn't want to upset the children. Upon arriving at the ear doctor's office, I felt weak, almost faint. I knew what I was about to see was not good news, and suddenly I wanted to walk, maybe even run, the other way. The doctor had already put the films up for viewing.

I sat down, and he explained, in his clinical way, that I had a tumor behind my eye that was about four and one-half centimeters. I looked at the picture and could not believe it was that big. How could I have something like that and not know it?

"Linda, I want you to walk over to the emergency room with these films. The doctors over there are waiting to talk to you."

I already knew which one I wanted for my surgeon, but questions flooded my mind. Will this be cancerous? Who will take care of the kids? How am I going to manage? Entering the emergency area, I was met by a slew of doctors that I already knew. A couple of them hugged me, knowing what I must have been going through at that moment. I knew that all of them sympathized with me. I made an appointment with one of the best surgeons in town.

Walking into the surgeon's office three days later, I noticed other people in the waiting room. Some of them could hardly walk, and others had bandages. At that moment, I looked perfectly well.

You can't judge a book by its cover. I sat down and waited for what seemed like an eternity. "Hi Linda," the surgeon said, "let's talk about what this means."

The next few minutes were the worst minutes of my life.

"Linda, first of all, this surgery will take a very long time. That means I will have to be on my feet for ten to twelve hours or more. I must take a vacation to rest before I do this."

At that moment, I could not believe what I was hearing. He wanted to take a vacation. What? Doesn't he know that this is all about me? I have to walk around with this thing in my head, and he is going on vacation? I was so upset, yet I knew that I wanted him to do a good job. If this meant a vacation, I could not complain. The next part of the briefing was not encouraging.

"Linda, fatality for this is possible. You need to go home and take care of things."

Preparing to die was not what I had in mind, yet I knew I must tell the children. How would I feel if I left this world? Taking my rose-colored diary out of the drawer, I thought about what it would be like to have the children hold it after I was gone. Tears flooded my eyes, and I started to write:

> *To my beloved children*
>
> *Cara, Phillip, Rebecca, and Elena*
>
> *You are my children, and no matter if I am here or where I am, I will always be your mother. You will remain in my heart forever. Never forget the wonderful years we have spent together and the things we have taught each other. Be proud of who you are, not what others want you to be.*
>
> *Always look to God for comfort, for he will never forsake you. Never forget the love we had for each other, no matter what we went through.*

Please put each other first and be there to pick each other up when needed. Remember to keep your family first and foremost, and in the end, love is the only thing that will count.

My beautiful girls, I love you all the same, but differently, because you were uniquely made. If I could, I would take you with me. That would be a selfish act, as you have so much life to live and to give. You are all so precious. What does a mother say to her children if she knows she might die? I am saying what I know my mother would have said to me if she had known she was going to leave me:

I love you with all my heart, and I have raised you to be proud of the woman you are and will become. I am especially proud, as I know each one of you has a part of me. Do not let the event of my death affect your life; live the rest of yours to the fullest. No matter where you go, carry me in your hearts. Persist in making a difference in the world that you live in. Be happy knowing I will be in a much better place.

To my beloved son Phillip:

You, my son, are special. You are my only son. I am proud of your accomplishments and the man you have become. Take care of your sisters and be there when they need you. Don't forget the special bond that only mothers and sons can have. You have done well with your life, and always remember that God is with you. If I leave this world, in my heart, you will go with me. Many times, I found comfort in your quiet and loving ways.

You have a calm and gentle spirit. I pray it never leaves you. Remember, son, my spirit will remain with you forever. Remember to look to God for strength in times of trouble. I love you all. Your beloved mother.

By my second visit to the doctor, I knew that I had to break the news to them.

Believe me, this is not what a mother wants to tell her children. Already, Cara was full term and had been to the hospital three times in false labor. I was hoping she would have the baby before I had my surgery.

Walking into the house, I looked at all of them. There was Elena, my baby girl. What a precious baby she was. She was so sweet and sensitive, always wanting to please me with what she did. My heart twinged with pain as I thought of telling her my news. One by one, I took them into the bedroom and talked privately to them. First, I began with, "You know how much Mommy loves you. I need to tell you something, and I need you to be strong for me and for all of us. It is OK to cry, though.

By then, a worried look would cross their faces. What I remember most is when I told Elena. She was the youngest, and I worried so much for her. "Mommy, I don't want to hear this, she told me in a little girl's voice.

Elena's Story

When I was six years old, I told myself I was going to be a movie star. In my imagination, I would make billions of dollars. People were supposed to cater to my every need. My enormous imagination often got me into trouble in school. Teachers were worried I was spending too much time gazing out the window and not enough time with my head in the books. I had beautiful dreams. The only problem was that I didn't want to work for them. I felt that things would be handed to me on a silver platter without hesitation. I just knew other people would always be there for me. This train of thought came to a screeching halt after something unexpected took place.

It was a cold December morning. The air was crisp, and the trees whistled in the wind. I was playing outside with a couple of neighbors, and I turned around to hear the muffled call of my mother's voice. I then looked up at the beautiful blue sky and dreaded leaving its presence, for when I returned, it might be gone. I walked sadly into the house, pouting and stomping my feet. I took my heavy winter coat and dropped it on the floor. I knew this would make her angry. She reached for my hand, and I reluctantly gave it to her. I felt her hand squeeze mine tightly as she led me up the stairs and into her bedroom. She looked around for a couple of seconds, as if puzzled about what to say. My mother then sat down on her fluffy white bedspread. I loved that bedspread. I remember wanting one, but my mother told me I would only get it dirty. She grabbed my other hand and told me that there was something important she wanted to tell me. I remained standing because I knew my friends were waiting outside impatiently. Then I noticed something. Her eyes were sad and puffy, like she had been crying. But my mother didn't cry! She was strong!

I looked at her, confused, as she began speaking. She told me she had been to the doctor the other day, and they found a tumor in her brain and were going to try and take it out. My heart started racing. I tried to say something, but I couldn't talk. There were no words to express how I felt. It wasn't possible that my mother, my only mother, could die. Who would take care of me? Who would give me soup when I was sick and stay with me until I fell asleep? After these disturbing thoughts crossed my mind, I erased them, then said,

"Mom, don't tell me this."

That was all I could and would say. It was too unbearable to think that no one would be there to care for me. Then I unclenched my hands from hers and walked away before another word was spoken....

The next few weeks had everyone walking softly. I often went to the college near us and spent time playing the piano. This was a wonderful time of solace. My connection with God was so strong, and as time went on, I felt that I was going to be just fine. I was still apprehensive but had a calmness that had settled over me that I couldn't describe. I made sure we had a Christmas tree. Our Christmases as a family were always special. This tree was very tall and big. The girls strung popcorn, and I watched as they laughed and chattered. I looked at them. This could very well be my last Christmas with them. I must cherish this moment forever.

I would catch them staring at me and see the sad look on their faces. I knew how much they loved me, and I just didn't know how I could ever let them go. Every night, I prayed. Lord, please heal my body and keep my children from stress. I knew they were all in so much emotional pain. They started to mourn my loss. Rebecca expressed her emotions so vividly in a poem she wrote.

Rebecca's Poem

PAINFULLY SILENCED

The laughs that we last shared have perished
into a world of silence.
Memories fade with each passing day,
the blackness succumbs them.
The shadows won't last,
but the cry of endless suffering, never escaping.
One last breath eases the pain.
banishing the fear we run from.
Obstacles flood the paths,
Miles, so it is difficult to run without drowning.
Meaningless suffering that seals the passion for the air we breathe,
following broken paths like blind bats.
Trails of echoes racing through the mind,
thoughts ringing over and over.
Time won't heal the wounds,
until they are surfaced and the air braises them.
Pain must be driven from its place of comfort,
so freedom can rise to its rightful throne.
Rebecca Montoya

The children tried to make this our best Christmas ever. We all knew this could be my last Christmas.

Cara was still hanging on to that grandchild. The doctor told her it was because she had to know if I was going to live before the baby was born. I worried about her. She had always been the responsible one because she was the oldest. I knew she felt terrible about me, and she was miserable carrying the baby. My surgery was set for January 15, and the baby was due weeks before that. For some reason, the doctor did not want to start Cara's labor.

Cara's Journal

Dec. 12, 1990

It has been a couple of days since I last wrote in here, and I guess I didn't know exactly how to express all the feelings I have at this moment. The other day started as it always did, with me getting up and being agitated because I want this baby now! My day got much worse when my mother said she had something to tell me and I could not tell anyone else. She looked very solemn, and I asked, "What is it?"

The next hour or so was probably the most devastating I have faced so far. My mom has a brain tumor. She is going to have surgery next month. What am I supposed to say to that? I am mad. I feel numb. I still can't totally explain everything I am feeling.

It was 2:00a.m., and I could not sleep. Remembering that day as two strangers entered my home as a child to take my real mother, visions of hospital sheets and men in white coats were haunting me. I turned and saw the shape of a young man on the floor next to my bed. It was my teenage son. He did not know that I knew he was there, for he would slip away before I woke up. He was so special. A very sensitive boy who is always willing to help me. I always wondered what he felt, but he was not good at communicating his thoughts and feelings. It was more evident in the things he did. Seeing him next to me on the floor made me know how he felt about what was about to happen.

Phillip's Story

I was only sixteen at the time of Mom's surgery. It was such a terrible time. I couldn't stand seeing her this way. I remember her telling me, and I just stood there in shock. I could not believe this could happen to my mom. Our family is strong, and we all pulled through it together. It hurt my heart to see my mother like this. Mom's strength and courage gave us what we needed to go through the worst time that I can remember.

All I remember about Christmas 1990 were the lights on the tree. We all sat around staring, and nobody wanted to talk.

Dec. 16, 1990

Well, another day, and I feel like I'm going to break down. My mom said her doctor told her to come home and prepare in the event she does not make it. That must mean her chances are not good. This is not happening. My mom cannot die. She is the only mom I have, and she is my best friend. I am having her first grandchild, and she has to be here. My mom is being so strong, and I am trying to be for her too, but my insides are being torn apart. I know that the only way for me to deal with this is to go on as if everything is the same, but really, how do I do that because it's not?

Dec. 18, 1990

Today I woke up and couldn't feel my arms. I am so tired of being pregnant. Mom got up and massaged my arms until I could feel them again. She is going through so much right now, yet she still worries about me. I could never have gotten through the last several months without her. How can I even think of going through my life without having Mom in it? We still sit and talk about what it is going to be like when a baby comes, as if everything is almost normal. But we all know it is not. We all know that this has changed our lives forever.

But we are still unsure what the future holds for us. We have all been so close. Mom is the one who holds us together, and her love just keeps us going.

Dec. 19, 1990

I am having a moment. I am having a hard time finding time to sit down and write. That used to be a better part of my day. I spend more time worrying about what the future holds for me and my family. I can't imagine how my sisters are feeling. Becky and Lena walk around like they don't really know exactly what is going on, and Phillip, well, I think he is either in denial or is one very strong boy. He keeps telling me not to worry. Mom is going to be fine. Every time he sees that worried look on my face, he must know what I am thinking. He tells me calmly not to worry. Christmas is right around the corner, and it does not feel very Christmas-like around our house.

Dec. 21, 1990

Today I am going to buy Mom presents. I am not sure what to get her; I've never had this problem before. I am thinking of some cozy slippers. Then she can wear them in the hospital. I want her to be as comfortable as possible. I am miserable. I keep having false labor.

I bought the slippers for Mom. Sitting in the parking lot, I looked over at them and began to cry. I was remembering mom's little feet and how she surprised me on my 18th birthday. I knew it was her because I saw her little feet walking under the divider. I was crying so hard that I couldn't stop. It has suddenly hit me. I may lose Mom, and I only have a few more weeks to make as many memories as I can. This will be the best Christmas we've ever had.

Dec. 25, 1990

Well, it's Christmas! I can't exactly say it's the best. But it wasn't bad. Mom really liked all her presents. It was just wonderful spending time with mom, hugging her, and laughing with her. We all tried to have fun, but I think it was hard for all of us. At least it was for me. My heart breaks every time I look at her and see the fear in her eyes. Mom shows us her strength. God, why is this happening to her? Please, please just let her make it through this, and we will deal with whatever comes after that. That is all I ask. Just help her make it through the surgery and give her strength for what she has to go through. Help us deal with the fact that we might lose her. What are we going to do without her?

Jan. 1, 1991

OK, I can't deal with this anymore. Being pregnant and now overdue, I am angry, sad, and really confused. This baby is supposed to be here, and Mom only has fourteen days left until her surgery. I want my baby here before then. The surgery is getting closer, and I am getting more tense. I think I need to go hug Mom and talk to her for a while.

Jan. 2, 1991

I am now thirteen days overdue and very frustrated. Mom is getting ready to go to the hospital, and I am trying to be strong for her because the last thing she needs is to see me falling apart. I love Mom so much. She always knows just the right thing to say at the perfect time. She says that everything is going to be all right and that she will be home in a few weeks because her doctor is the best. I pray that she is right.

The next few weeks flew by. I had to go into the doctor's office every two days to make sure that water was not building up on the brain. If so, they would have to go in and drain it. I prayed that would not happen.

I packed my suitcase the day before the surgery. All the children were ready to go with me to the hospital. We got in the car and commented that we wanted this ride to last a very long time.

Elena's Story

That dreadful day in January came when we were to say goodbye to our mother before the surgery. The thought of this day made me sick to my stomach. What would I say to her?

I got out of bed and began getting dressed. My thoughts were scattered like jumbled knots. I knew this might be the last day that I ever spoke to my mother.

I hesitantly walked outside to the car, where everyone was waiting for me. I was wedged in between my sister and brother in the silver Chevy Nova. During the long ride to the hospital, I thought selfishly about who was going to look after me. When I remembered everyone else, I became aware of the silence that consumed us. We all suffered in silence.

I could see the hospital in view up ahead. My heart began beating faster as we approached the tall, yellow building. As we pulled up the driveway, my heart began to hurt. It was time to say goodbye, and I didn't know how to do it. I never intended to go this far without telling her that I loved her.

We got out of the car and walked into the lobby of the hospital. There weren't very many people there. I had expected to see the halls flooded with tons of sick people. I hadn't been to a hospital before that I could remember. The lights were dim, and the place was entirely quiet. I gazed at my mother and I saw the same sadness I'd seen when I looked into her eyes one month ago. I wanted to comfort her, but I didn't know how. This was all very new to me, and I was still in shock.

When my mother was ready to go into surgery, we all got to say something to her. I walked into her room and looked at the tired woman who lay on the bed.

She looked back at me and gave me a little grin. Her eyes drooped, and I could tell she was going to fall asleep soon. I knew it was now or never. Before I could speak, she told me to be quiet. She whispered, "Sweetheart, it will all be alright."

I knew she was only trying to make me feel better. I held her hand and reached over to give her a kiss on her soft skin. That was the last time I ever saw my mother the way she once was...

Walking through the corridors, I could smell the antiseptic and see the blur of white coats. How many times had I taken care of patients for the same things I was going in for? It was as if I was praying constantly. Even in my waking hours. My stepmother and family had called me several times to reassure me that they were praying for me as well. At this time, the only thing I had to hold on to was God and my children. They were everything to me.

A woman's voice said, "Here is your gown." She was the night nurse. Her clipboard was in her hand, and she looked like she was prepared for her shift.

"Linda, how are you feeling, and do you need something for pain?" "No, I am fine; thank you."

I knew I would probably need something to sleep, but I decided to wait for that. I had brought my little tape recorder with praise tapes to listen to for comfort.

Lying in my bed, my whole life must have passed before me. I remembered the look on my children's faces as they left the hospital. I knew the torture they felt, but I had come to terms with the fact that I was no longer in control. I had to give my will and my life to God. He had always had it, but I just did not know how much until now. All those years of church in my youth were surely helpful at this moment.

Drifting in and out of sleep, suddenly I felt a rustle in the sheets on my bed. Startled, I almost jumped. I felt the pressure of a warm hand pressing on mine. I looked down, and kneeling there on the side of my bed was a nurse that looked like a nun dressed in blue and white. I heard her softly praying.

"Lord, keep your hand on Linda and bless her. Do not let any harm come to her. . ." This continued on for ten minutes.

When she got up to leave, I wanted to ask her who she was, but she left before I could speak to her. I found this strange but very comforting. I looked at the clock, and it was 2:15 a.m. I dropped back into sleep and was awakened by what I thought were the drapes being drawn. The clock read 3:00 a.m.

I looked over to that corner of the room and saw a light and the shape of a door standing there as if to comfort me. This night was becoming very strange and almost frightening. I would have been afraid, but I have always been taught to believe that God shows himself in mysterious ways.

This light was very comforting. I felt like I was being shown something, but I did not know what. To this day, I do not know who or what those two incidents were about, but I believe they were sent for my comfort in a desperate time of need.

It was 6:00 a.m. They brought the gurney into my room and said, "OK, we are ready, are you?"

"No," I said. They all just laughed. Downstairs, I was left in the hall before going into surgery. Another nurse came by, and at that time she recited the Lord's Prayer. I thanked her for her concern. This hospital was not affiliated with any church, yet it seemed as if this power was being drawn to me.

I was well aware of what I would see in the surgery room. I already knew what was about to take place, and I spoke the lingo.

"Hey guys, put me under before you put in the NG tube (a plastic tube through my nose) and shave my head. I don't want to know what's going on.

"Ok, will do."

The anesthesiologist inserted the needle into my arm, and off into dreamland I went. There was no time to think about living or dying.

As I woke up in the ICU, a light beamed into my eye. It was Dr. Don, a local orthopedist. I had previously managed his office, and he had come to check out my situation. I can remember thinking, You are alive! If I had not been so sick to my stomach, I would have been dancing on the ceiling! My head ached and my stomach felt like I was on a ship in the worst tide, but I was alive. ***Thank you, God!***

Jan. 16, 1991

It has been about a week since my last entry here, and a lot has happened.

Where do I start? Mom went into surgery, and I was pacing nervously for what seemed like a lifetime. It lasted from the morning until nighttime. I had so many things going through my head. I was so tired and still had not had my baby. I couldn't believe I was three weeks overdue, but that day I wasn't thinking about that. The only thing I could think of was my mom. I kept repeating to myself that ***she was going to be alright****. But, for some reason, I did not believe what I was saying. I felt so unsure. I tried to prepare myself for when the doctor appeared. It finally happened. The doctor came to the waiting area, and boy, did he look tired! I actually held my breath and waited to hear what he had to* *say. "She made it, and she is hanging in there," he told us. I felt so overwhelmed and so happy! I have my mom! I just wanted to see her so badly. The doctor took my brother Phil and me to the ICU unit. I definitely was not prepared for what I saw. It broke my heart to see my mom with a bandage on her head and no hair. It really wasn't that, but she looked so frail, like if I touched her, she would break. I wanted to hug and comfort her, but I was afraid to touch her. She looked at me and whispered,*

"Go have that baby."

She was still worried about the rest of us. As my brother and I left the hospital, I finally broke down and started to shake and cry. I could no longer contain my composure.

"It's OK, Cara," Phillip said, and he hugged me until I felt better. Then he drove me to the military hospital, I checked in, and I became the proud mother of a beautiful baby boy. His name is Shayne Phillip.

Two of my children were at my bedside. Cara was bigger than I had ever seen her, and Phillip was the only one allowed in the ICU. Judging by the look on their faces, I must have looked pretty bad. I could hardly talk, but they kissed me, and I told Cara to go have her baby. And that is what she did. The very next day, my first grandchild was born.

The days following were days of pain and agony, but the fact that I was alive made them worth living. I had no idea what lay ahead. I knew I had a grandchild and was so happy. I just wanted to get well in a hurry. Everyone who knows me knows I have no patience, and I want it "yesterday."

The nurses in the ICU (Intensive Care Unit) had been chosen with the greatest of care. They were kind, caring, and very careful not to do anything that would be uncomfortable. My arms were black and blue from the needle pricks and my rolling veins that curled up when needles were stuck in them. The doctors were alarmed at viewing them, too. I put them at ease. "This always happens! My veins love to roll!" I said.

On my second day in the hospital, I was moved to the floor out of the ICU. It was very difficult to even move. My head seemed attached to my stomach, and they were both very sick. When I could sleep, it was on a towel curled around my neck. Nothing could touch my head. Nurses and doctors were amazed that I was taking only aspirin for a brain surgery. I knew I had a high pain tolerance, and at this time, I was very thankful.

The scar went from the top of my head past the nape of my neck. The doctor had performed a craniotomy, which consisted of drilling a hole in my skull in order for the brain to be retracted. The days of recovery were long, and getting out of bed for the first time was going to be a very bad experience. I have memories of my doctors standing over me and talking as if I were not in the room.

"Well, so far, so good, but we know how these things can turn," he said. They were concerned about things like blood clotting and seizures taking place after the surgery.

It was 6:00 p.m., and the night shift (6:00 p.m.-2:00 a.m.) had been briefed. Of course, I still had a Foley catheter, and I had not been out of bed as yet. They had not served me solid food yet, and I had just had surgery the day before. The nurse, big and looking like she hated the night shift, walked into my room at 5:15. She said,

"Girl, you are getting out of bed today!"

I was shocked at this, as I was too weak to really walk in them. The doctors were alarmed at viewing them, too. I put them at ease. "This always happens! My veins love to roll!" I said.

On my second day in the hospital, I was moved to the floor out of the ICU. It was very difficult to even move. My head seemed attached to my stomach, and they were both very sick. When I could sleep, it was on a towel curled around my neck. Nothing could touch my head. Nurses and doctors were amazed that I was taking only aspirin for a brain surgery. I knew I had a high pain tolerance, and at this time, I was very thankful.

The scar went from the top of my head past the nape of my neck. The doctor had performed a craniotomy, which consisted of drilling a hole in my skull in order for the brain to be retracted. The days of recovery were long, and getting out of bed for the first time was going to be a very bad experience. I have memories of my doctors standing over me and talking as if I were not in the room.

"Well, so far, so good, but we know how these things can turn," he said. They were concerned about things like blood clotting and seizures taking place after the surgery.

It was 6:00 p.m., and the night shift (6:00 p.m.-2:00 a.m.) had been briefed. Of course, I still had a Foley catheter, and I had not been out of bed as yet. They had not served me solid food yet, and I had just had surgery the day before. The nurse, big and looking like she hated the night shift, walked into my room at 5:15. She said,

"Girl, you are getting out of bed today!"

I was shocked at this, as I was too weak to really walk and I still had a catheter. She came to my bed, took my hand, and jerked me as if pulling me out of the bed. I could not believe this. I had been a nurse for so many years, and I knew something was very wrong. Weakly, I demanded,

"Leave me alone. I want my doctor."

The next thing I knew, another nurse had entered my room, apologizing for the first nurse's actions. Apparently, she had me mixed up with the lady in the next room. I was a very unhappy patient.

The next morning, it was "off to the tube once again." They had to check how the surgery went by giving me an MRI. This time, I really thought my days were numbered. I could not move. My head swam, and I was constantly sick to my stomach. I begged and I pleaded. "Please don't move me! I won't make it in there! I will have to throw up."

They must have heard the urgency in my voice. My whole bed went with me as I was wheeled down the hall. I knew I was alive, but would I live through this? The two guys welcomed me into the room. I could give them only a faint smile. "Ok, let's put a sheet under her, and when I say pull, move… They began to move me. My head swam, and as I turned it sideways," I thought, "God, I am so sick."

Despite getting sick all over the technicians, I did live through it. Laying in the familiar "tub," I began to think how thankful I was to be alive and able to be in "the tube." This session went more quickly than I expected.

CHAPTER X

A New Look and a New Life

The next day, when I was able to sit up, the nurse asked me, "Linda, would you like to comb your hair and look at yourself in the mirror?"

Didn't she know I had no hair? Cruel, very cruel.

This scared me, as I knew I would not look like myself. Strange feelings came from my face. I had a difficult time talking and noticed I couldn't smile. Since I am one to face the music, I said, "sure." There was no hair, the right side of my face drooped, my right eye would not close, and I was completely deaf in the right ear with the same terrible high-pitched ringing that I had before surgery. I looked in the mirror, and I wanted to die. I had no idea that I would be praying that prayer in the weeks to come, but that is exactly what happened.

After three days at the hospital, the doctor was surprised that I wanted to go home. This is not usually done, but I have always considered myself a fast healer. I was dreading my trip home because it was torture to move. I did not know how the children would take this, as Cara had just had the baby, and I did not look like the mother that left our home a few days earlier.

Stepping out of the car, I felt like I was missing something and was walking with only half my head on my shoulders. That tumor must have been pretty large for me to be missing it.

I knew I had to walk up a flight of stairs, but I was so happy to be home and alive. I knew my new grandchild was awaiting my touch. I had sung to him and talked to him before he was born. I wondered how connected I would feel.

Elena's Story

The news of the successful surgery came that same day. I was relieved to hear that my mother was going to be coming home in a couple of weeks. I was sitting on the couch watching cartoons one morning when my older sister sat next to me and said she wanted to talk to me about how things would be when mommy came home.

I was sitting on the couch playing with my new baby doll that I had gotten for Christmas. The wind chimes clinked together like bells in the air. The wind blew like soft whispers that were singing to me. I began biting my nails and looking nervously around the room. Then I stood up and started pacing the floors, walking back and forth and glancing out the window every now and then. The thought of what was to come sent chills up my spine. I sat back down on the big fluffy couch and began to mumble a tune beneath "Under the Weeping Willow Tree."

My breath that my mother used to sing to me sometimes. "Strawberry shortcake is my friend; she will love me till the end." I pictured my mother here with me, cradling me in her warm embrace and rocking me as I rocked my baby doll. I could hear her soothing voice as I sang.

Jan. 18, 1991

Cara's Journal

Finally, I am home. That was the longest four days of my life! Shayne is so cute and sweet. I wish I could take him to see Mom. She would be so proud. He doesn't sleep much, so I am really having a hard time. I feel like I could sleep standing up. Mom is holding her own. She is not herself yet, but I am thankful she is still very much a part of our lives.

All four children waited at the top of the stairs. My friend held one arm, and I shuffled as I walked. Reaching the last stair was the most difficult. I really did not want them to see me like this; I was so weak and did not look like the mother they knew. When I took that final step, they were all terrified and as they all hugged me, I saw Elena, my youngest. She exhibited such fear. My appearance will startle them, I knew. But I realized that, in time, we could all pull through this. Everything in due time.

Elena's story

The car door slammed, and I heard a faint voice say, "Are you OK? Do you need some help, Mom?"

My eyes widened, and I clenched my teeth. The front door slowly opened with a creak, then slammed like thunder. I jumped up and ran back to the window. There I saw my sister's silver Dodge clunker with the ignoramus dent in the rear bumper. I quickly ran back to the couch and sat down. I grabbed my doll with my shaky hands and held her tightly to comfort myself. Footsteps slowly creaked up the stairs. My eyes widened as I jerked my head in the direction of the stairs. My heart started beating faster and faster. I began to breathe harder and harder. The footsteps got louder as they reached the top. Then I saw her…

She slowly limped her way toward me, and I slowly backed away. I cautiously looked her up and down to see what had become of my mother. She wore a cap that covered the monstrous scar that went up the back of her head. Looking in my direction, she said, "Hello, my little one."

My heart raced as I stared at her face, which seemed to be half-motionless when she mumbled those four little words to me. My frightened eyes looked away, but something drew me back. My mother's pale, tired face looked up at me. I then looked into her empty eyes, and she glanced away. I saw an unusual sadness about her that she had never shown. I looked at the stranger who stood before me, and my heart began to hurt. An overwhelming sadness came over me, and one single tear fell from my eye and rolled down my cheek. My palms were sweating, and I felt their stickiness as I nabbed them together.

I glanced at my sister, who was staring back at me with a worried look on her face. She looked the way I felt. A stream of tears began running down her cheeks, and a burst of uncontrollable emotions came out of her. She ran to me, and her arms reached for me. The tightness of her hug caused me to lose my breath, so I pushed her away. I glanced at the stranger whom I called mother, and once again I saw that sadness deep within her eyes. She sat down and closed her eyes, like it was the first time she had closed her eyes in weeks. Her tired, drained body sank into the couch cushions. My sister Cara whispered in a soft, low voice, "Lena, go and give her a hug. She loves you, and she's scared, too."

I slowly walked to my mother and reached my shaking arms out toward her. I longed for her warm, snug embrace around my shaky body. I leaned over nervously and hugged her tightly. I could feel her weak hands wrapping around me. I felt her try to squeeze tight. I squeezed her until the strength in my arms was gone. Her hug felt warm and loving. My face dug into her shoulder, and the smell of hospital from her gown filled my nostrils. The feeling of warmth inside the room gave me a sense of relief. I tilted my head up so that I could see my mother's face. She had an innocence about her that made her look childlike. She wore a big, crooked smile that seemed to go up the whole side of her face. The love I felt from that smile warmed my heart and told me how much she loved me. I had felt afraid, hurt, sad, and weak in this situation. I felt useless. But that smile vanquished all the fears inside of me. My mother was home, and that was all that mattered. I realized that we would all get through this together. Through love, we would make it all possible. Sure, my life would never be the same, but at least I wasn't going to be living it without my mother.

Entering the bedroom, I saw a tiny figure lying in a crib. I shuffled as I walked, feeling like I was 90 years old. Reaching the crib, I could not believe my eyes! My grandson was the most beautiful, perfect child I had ever seen. Love, joy, and happiness flooded my heart as I bent over to kiss his cheek.

"I am home, my love, and I am alive," I whispered.

I could not pick him up because I had no strength, but instead I cried tears of joy as I put my hand over his little chest. I felt a strong heartbeat. Hearing the cries of a newborn baby was a joyful noise to me.

Cara's Journal

Jan. 20, 1991

Yesterday, Mom came home. Boy, was I surprised! She was supposed to be in the hospital for a few weeks. I am so happy she is home. We helped her up the stairs, and she went straight to Shayne's crib. Her first grandchild was there, so tiny and precious. It broke my heart that she was too weak to hold him. She stood there and cried. I could see the pain on her face, and I could feel it. That was a moment I will never forget.

Jan. 25, 1991

Mom has been home for a while, and my life has been so hectic. I can't seem to find the time to write here anymore. Mom is so fragile, and it is so hard to watch what she is going through. I can't imagine being in her place and losing so much of my life, plus having to start over. I know it must be really hard for her to have to let me take care of her. She is like a child, revealing so many things. I pace the floors at night with her, wishing this was just a bad dream.

Between Mom and Shayne, I am not sleeping, and I feel like I can't do this anymore. How much more can I take? I feel agitated. I know it's not Mom's fault that she is going through this. Her medication keeps her up at night. I am constantly giving her ice chips. When I bathe her, I feel overwhelmed with emotion; this is my mother. I love her so much. This is the way it happens. Our parents raise us and provide for us, and eventually the roles are reversed. But now, this should not be happening, and it is not fair that she has to go through this. My brother is in denial. Becky and Lena did not grasp the whole thing until they saw Mom after her surgery. I just feel so overwhelmed, and I want to scream. I feel it inside; I just can't get it out. Seeing her like this is tearing me apart inside.

Cara was a very loving child, and now she was a mother. It was so enjoyable to watch her care for and love her child as much as I did. I knew it took an enormous amount of her strength to care for me and her newborn baby as well. This did not seem to affect her nursing the baby, but I feared it might. I watched her as she washed me, cared for me, and walked with me at night when I could not sleep. She did this so unselfishly, with great amounts of love and devotion.

In this, I learned a great lesson in giving. I found it difficult to lay back and let them care for me. Daily, I was being healed slowly with large doses of love. Every day the children would somehow touch me, telling me that they loved me and that I would be better soon.

Just as I thought things were getting a little better, my chest felt as though it was caving in. It was a traumatic time. I was not sleeping but walking the floor nightly because of the medication I took for swelling of the brain. It was very difficult because I was too weak to get out of bed. I was miserable and vomited every morning. This ritual continued for about three months. There were times that I felt death might take me to a much better place. I continued to pray for strength.

Late one night, I had a strange feeling in my chest. I couldn't breathe and hardly had the strength to walk. I knew I had to go to the emergency room and called Phillip to take me there. It was 3:00 a.m. He was up in no time and ready to help me to the car. I wondered what could possibly be wrong. I had brain surgery, but nothing to do with my chest!

Walking into the emergency room, I saw a room full of people. The sign hung on the door: "Emergencies are taken according to need." Well, I know that at a time like this, everyone feels they have the greatest need.

The girl at the desk asked me why I was there. "I just had brain surgery, and I can't breathe."

"You can't breathe, and you had brain surgery?" She was amused. I was getting a little upset.

"I need to see the doctor right now."

"I know, I know; just take a seat and we will call you." I had worked in the ER, and I knew the drill. This was real education from the other side.

"Is Dr. Crow working tonight?" I asked.

"Oh," you know him, she said. "Yes," I said.

"Ok, I will check."

It's not what you know; it's who you know.

"No, he is not working, but the other doctor is, and he will see you." I was thankful, and I walked down the hallway on Phil's arm.

Speaking with the physician, I found out that I had an infection from the tube during surgery. I was thankful and relieved that it was nothing more serious.

What could be more serious than brain surgery?

The love that my children gave me during this time was far beyond any that I have ever known. I would lay there and watch them take care of the bills, the washing, the car, the groceries, and everything else that needed to be done. I felt pride in the strength they showed me. I knew that I had taught them well, and yet, at the same time, I knew this was a labor of love that they were giving to me. There is no greater love than this, except for God's love.

I watched Cara with her new baby and wondered how she was going to make it taking care of me and the baby. This was unbelievable. My children healed me with their love. Every day, I was met with hugs and kisses, telling me that they were the luckiest kids in the world to have me as their mother. Feeling my warm, squirming little grandson on my lap made my life worth living.

One morning I awoke to the sounds of clanging dishes and the rustle of crisp, clean sheets being shaken. Cara was making the bed, and the girls were laughing. I knew it was just about time for a birthday cake, and this year, I was approaching my forty-third birthday in a much calmer fashion. It had been two months since my surgery, and every day was a little better. The kids knew that my greatest fear was going out into a world where I had no hair. As a child, I was properly raised and conditioned to believe that presentation was everything. How could I be presentable when my face drooped, I could not smile, and I had no hair? I felt like a freak of nature. That familiar feeling I had as a child was back again. The children bought me bright-colored handkerchiefs to match what I wore. They knew this was my worst nightmare.

It was exceptionally quiet in the house on my birthday. As night approached, there was a wonderful smell in our kitchen. The girls were making cake. I received a very special birthday surprise that night. Something that I needed but was very afraid to try. They bought a blonde wig that looked just like my hair. I felt natural wearing it, and I was getting ready to be seen. Time was passing, and I had to start making decisions. I knew my disability insurance would run out soon, and there would be no money.

Three months later, my brother, Jimmy, came from Washington, D. C., to see for himself how "really" I was. The look on his face told me what he thought, but he was trying to be happy, and he said, "I know what you need —a nice ride to Carmel Beach.

This was my first time going outside since I came home in a car after my surgery. Off I went with my little handkerchief on my head, feeling like a freak of nature. This was very difficult, as being in the car was not easy. But he was the only family that I had been able to see besides the children. His love and support were very comforting.

It took me a year to recover from this surgery and its aftermath. I had lots of time to think about what my experience could offer me and others. My surgery left me with many residual problems, both emotionally and physically, which I knew I had to deal with. I was not the same woman in so many ways. Could I accept who I had become, and could I work with the new person I was? This was the greatest challenge of my entire life. Returning to my spirituality, I began to search for the reason for my experience and rejoice in the opportunities that I met.

CHAPTER XI

Living Imperfect in a Perfect World

A year had almost passed since my surgery, and my disability insurance was about to expire. I was wondering what I would do and how I would manage. I was definitely feeling better and thought it was time for me to start thinking about work. I had no idea where to start on this venture. I knew it was not going to be easy this time around, and I wondered how people would receive me.

It was Saturday, and the sun was shining through my window. This is the day.

Pulling myself out of bed was not as difficult as it had been in days past. I felt rejuvenated and alive. Opening my closet, I touched the clothes that had been unfamiliar to me for so long. It was as though I had a new wardrobe. This is going to be fun. Pulling down my favorite skirt and top, I felt the soft material as I slipped them on. How I had taken advantage of touch, taste, and smell.

I knew my life would never be the same.

Looking in the mirror, I tried to smile. How could I have lost the one thing that meant so much to me? My smile was gone. At first, I had hopes of it coming back, but it had been almost a year and it had not returned. This ringing in my ear was so bothersome. I could not even get to sleep on some nights. Quit whining. This certainly beats the odds!

My mind went to my grandson, Shayne, who was taking his first steps and smiling every time he saw me. We were so close, and the thought that I might not have experienced his birth filled my heart with grief.

Feeling crisp and clean, I went up the stairs to meet the children. I knew they would be surprised to see me up and dressed in my Sunday best. When I reached the stairs, they all looked in my direction and did a double take.

"Mom, you look beautiful, Where are 'we' going?" "Well," I said. It is where 'I' am going." I was presented with disapproving looks and a lot of resistance.

"Mom, I don't think you are ready yet." "Sure, hon, it's only been a year, you know."

We all laughed. It was difficult for the children to give up their caregiving rituals. The car, the bills, and the house had been theirs for quite a while now. I held out my hand and said,

"Keys, please!"

Cara put them ever so gently in my hand, saying, "Please, be careful, mom."

This was amusing for me to watch. They were having a very difficult time giving me my independence back. I was excited about getting out and doing some things on my own, but I never dreamed that a new and different life awaited me, and I would have to take some very important steps to accept who I had been compared to who I was now.

Knowing nothing else but the medical field, I set out to get my first job.

The doctors will understand. But I went from doctor to doctor. I was not the Linda they knew a year before. I remember the horrified look on their faces. Even they were having a difficult time accepting me for the person I had become. It was most difficult because I could not smile or respond like the old Linda. Those days were long past. No doctor would want to set me up in his front office. I would not be able to greet patients with a smile.

My smile came from within.

I felt pretty lucky when a neurologist in town gave me a job. I was good at work ethics and professional enough for them to like my demeanor. They put me in a back office to work and gave me a desk. I was even allowed to structure my job. This was wonderful for me, and I was happy. Well, for a while. As I began to look better and my hair grew out, people seemed to think that I was OK. They began to give me more and more work to do. I felt stressed and did not realize what I was putting myself through. I began to ask for what I needed. Less lighting and structured work without change every day were some of my requests. The girls in the office began complaining that I was using my disability as an excuse to get what I wanted. This was so difficult, as the office manager was agreeing with them.

I did not know how long I could go on like this, but, again, I had to work for our family. It was this job that made me see just how cruel people can be. When my father died, I was not allowed to go to his funeral. I was told that I would "lose my job" if I took off. The computer had been down, and there was more work than usual. Walking out to my car with the cold wind hitting my face, I thought about my father. I reflected on the days we spent together. My dad was the best dad ever. No one could ever take his place. He would be so sad that I was not there to say my goodbyes, and so was I. My heart was saddened to think I had to let him go. He had been a wonderful father.

That night, the children wrote their personal letters that would be put in the breast pocket of my father's suit as he lay in the casket. My contribution was a heart of flowers with each grandchild's name. His favorite picture of me as a little girl sat next to his head on the cream-colored satin cloth. The day of the funeral, my brother called me, and I heard the ceremony over the phone. As soft organ music played, I thought about the wonderful times I had shared with him over the years. This was the single most difficult thing I had ever done in my life, besides surviving brain surgery. Not only was I unable to say goodbye to my biological mother, but to my father as well. To this day, there is a hole in my heart where my father's vibrant spirit once lay. He will be missed forever.

These people who call themselves professionals are cruel.

CHAPTER XII

A Healing Touch

One bright Saturday morning, I answered the phone to the sound of a very deep voice. "Hello, my name is Jerry. Did you order some shoes from "Red Wing Shoes?"

"Yes," I replied.

"You may pick them up at any time," he told me.

"OK," I said. I did not think much about this, as I was so concerned about my job and my family.

Walking into the men's shoe store, I saw a man standing in front of the register. Nice; he is cute. He had black hair and a nice smile. "Hello, may I help you?" "You have some shoes for me; my name is Linda Madison.

Returning, he held the box in his hand.

He complimented the shoes, and I told him they were for my son.

Well, one thing led to another, and we ended up seeing each other. It had been a while since I'd had any male companionship. I had wondered if that would ever happen in my life again, and I felt that my looks would prevent it. From day one, the kids complained. "He never talks to us; he is not friendly; he doesn't do this or that."

I never listened to their complaints because a healing process was taking place in my life. My inner soul was being transformed by someone who made me see my potential.

It had been only a year since my surgery. Jerry was different, and he made me feel special. My looks were not as important to him as my heart. This man healed my heart and enabled me to know the woman I really was. It was through his acceptance of my physical appearance that I accepted myself. I have no idea where he is today, but it doesn't matter. People are put into our lives for a reason, and he was with me for a season and was gone just as fast as he came. This relationship lasted for one year.

During this time, I met a woman who was putting together a non-profit organization for chronic pain. I met with her, and we decided to do the non-profit together, as I wanted to deal with disability and brain injury. Her organization was called Chronic Pain Support Services, and mine was Central Coast Impairment Management. I put in many long hours doing paper work and learning how a non-profit organization works. I put many long hours into this, but the work was rewarding and enjoyable. However, on the down side, my son had been with his father for a while, and they were complaining about some of the things he was doing. They felt he was sick, but they could not get him to go to the doctor.

One Saturday evening, we were headed to San Jose to pick Phil up from the airport. Walking down the airport hall, I saw a tall man. His head was shaved, and he had on a long coat. This was not my son; I cried all the way home.

The next day, I began to look for help. Of course, the first place I went was to work. I thought a neurologist would know something. No one seemed to be able to give me answers. I took Phil to get a CT scan and an MRI. He was finally diagnosed with a mental illness. My girls were in a state of shock, and so was I. I immediately quit my position at the doctor's office and once again went to the system for help.

Sitting by the pool in our apartment, I watched as Phillip took a dive. He was a natural. Always athletic, he excelled at everything he did. He was always a sensitive, loving child, and that has never changed. Now, he was well over six feet tall with blonde hair and a muscular build. I began to daydream of the days when he was about ten years old. I would stand in front of the kitchen window, doing dishes. I watched him as he got off the school bus and walked around a circle that made a path to our house. He whistled as he carried his books and walked with purpose. The purpose was probably milk and cookies and to play with his pet cat. I would think that someday my son would grow into a special young man.

Holding the towel, I went to the edge of the pool. As he climbed out, there was that same familiar smile, and as I walked back to the apartment, I heard a faint whistle.

When Phil and I are alone together, we don't have to talk. We connect in a very special way, differently than most mothers and sons. That very dark place in my heart created by the loss of my mother has begun to shine with a glow so bright that it radiates throughout my whole being. My son struggles in life to be like all the rest, and I share in that struggle. Being in that familiar place at one time helps me to support, love, and be a very patient mother.

Undoubtedly, I was quite stressed. Leaving the Social Security office one day, I was hit by a semi- truck on the passenger side of the car. I was not hurt, but the car was totaled.

"Ms., Are you all right in there?" the fireman asked.

"Yes, I said, not believing that I was alive after seeing that semitruck. I was sore, and the car was in the middle of the intersection.

I lived through brain surgery; why shouldn't I live through this?

The car door was open just enough for me to slip through it. The fireman helped me out of the car, and I wobbled over to the side of the building.

"Are you hurt, or do you have any other medical problems we should know about?" At that point, I thought maybe I should tell him about my surgery".

"Well, about a year ago, I had brain surgery," I told him. At that point, this guy clasped his hand around my neck and slapped my body against the wall. "Don't move!" he shouted.

"Oh! I won't! This is the most fun I have had all week."

This was funny, no doubt. If he only knew what I had been through in my life so far.

Trauma seemed to be everywhere I looked. How would I get another car? How can I even get groceries? Eventually, it all worked out. Ike and Juan at "Ike's Quality Car" never let me down.

It was business as usual at our house.

"Who wants to go grocery shopping with me?" That was always a joke because none of the kids wanted to be seen with me using food stamps. They would sit in the car until I finished and then help. I understood how difficult this must be for them, but I was thankful that I had the system at such a needed time. The rent was due, and I was just starting on welfare. I did not know how I was going to do this. The worst thing that would happen is that we would get evicted, and that process takes a while. So I sat back and bided my time.

Walking into the local grocery store, I piled the basket as high as I could. Feeding the kids was something I enjoyed. I liked them to eat as healthy as possible, and food stamps offered me that. I found it embarrassing to use my food stamps because I had always been able to provide for the children, but I knew I was struggling and was thankful for the help. I walked up to the long line and took out my wallet. I always tried to stand in front of the person behind me so they couldn't see how I was paying.

Well, on this day, it was going to be different. The cashier said, in a very loud voice,

"What are you on food stamps?" Well, if there had been a hole, I would have crawled into it. She was making such a fuss, and I was being shamed in front of a whole line of people. I could not believe this.

I asked to speak to the store manager. Yes, I was dressed nicely, and I looked presentable. But that was part of the prim and proper thing in my youth. I never equated that with having a lot of money.

"Hello, is there a problem here?" The manager said "Yes, I would like to speak to you in private." I left my groceries, and there was a whole line of people waiting to tell that manager what I thought about this episode. I proceeded to tell him my situation and how much I did not appreciate how I did not appreciate this treatment. I also told him that I was going to write an article in the paper about the treatment I had received at his store. He was very sorry when I left him, and he pulled me to another line after he took that cashier off the floor. I never saw her again after that. The lesson from that day was, never to judge a person by their looks. We are not walking in their shoes.

Phil soon got better, and I realized that I should look for some permanent help. I filed for Social Security, and at the same time, I filed for Phillip. It did not take long for Phil to get on Medi-Cal; for me, it took a very long time. At this point, I felt like this must have been a bad dream. Going on welfare was not the plan for my life. I have always been a strong and resourceful woman. But I could not work at all if I were to get Social Security disability. I did not know how we were going to make it. It had been two months, and they were going to evict me. I opted for the last resort and called my second husband, Rebecca, and Elena's father.

"You've got to help me; I have no money to keep the kids." "What can I do?" he said.

Where the girls were concerned, he was always there if needed. He moved into the apartment where we were living, and I moved out. It was one of the most difficult things I ever did. I saw the look of pain on their faces as I left. Surely, I was letting go of the one thing that has kept me going all these years—my children.

Searching once again for answers, I turned to my friends. On the phone that night, I called Suzanne.

"Hello, Suzie. I need some help."

This was a very humbling experience. It is easy for me to identify with the single women of the world who are poverty-stricken.

"Hi Linda, how are you? Long time, no hear!"

I told Suzie my situation. As the kind and loving friend that she was, she took me in. A single mother living with her two children, she was working as a licensed clinical social worker, and doing well living in a three-bedroom house. Her home was not far from my children. I began working more in the non-profit for brain injury and started going to church with Suzanne. This offered me peace in a time of turmoil, and I began to hope and pray for relief.

Sitting in the pew on Sunday morning, I watched the sun shine through the beautiful stained glass windows. As I closed my eyes, reflections of my past were so vivid in my mind. Long blonde banana curls tied with a satin red bow lay perfectly on the collar of my frilly pink dress. The sounds of worship and singing rang from the church loft. Hands were raised and clapped. The ushers stood in the back with their crisp black suits as they greeted those at the door. Everything was perfect," I thought. Mom would be proud of me. I gazed at my shoes. They matched. I felt my hair and the way it curled around my shoulders just right. My earrings sparkled like the sun. Then, I touched my face. I was jolted into reality by my obvious imperfections.

As I opened my eyes, I felt a warm hand being placed gently on mine. She leaned over to me and said, "You are so beautiful today and every day after this." I gave a crooked smile to my friend and felt the warmth of her hand. It was then that I knew that my past losses were soon to be my future gains.

My childhood experiences are a treasured journey that made me the woman I am today. My search for happiness was found only when I surrendered to life as it was meant for me. Through the life-changing experience of disability, I now have peace and contentment in knowing who I am and rejoice in the woman I have become.

From left to right	Rebecca	Cara Lynee
	Linda	
	Alena	

Phillip

Sam and Dorothy

Focused and Driven

After my surgery, I had a lot of time to think about what the next step of my life would be. I had taken classes at the community college level and already had some credits. I signed up for classes a year after my surgery. It was a long journey, and I really did not know if I could do it. It was difficult, as I had to sign up with the disability office. Luckily, I was given an outstanding counselor. I had a year to go, and I was ready to get it over. I was ending my last semester when my counselor pulled me into her office one day. "Linda", she said, have you considered continuing your education?" N0000, not really, I said. Well, I think you should, and I have set up an appointment with your rehabilitation counselor. I was stunned, as I never thought I would go on to my bachelor's. After my meeting with rehabilitation, the date was set to go to San Francisco State.

I met my counselor in the community parking lot, and we started our journey to San Francisco State. I was quiet. "Linda," she said. It will be fine. The counselors there are very nice and accommodating. You will be very glad we made this trip".

I was afraid when I stepped out of the parking lot. It was a noticeably big campus with a lot of younger kids. I was already 50, so I was a late bloomer and scared of how I would ever get around on the big campus. Talking to the counselor, I set up my classes, and two weeks later I got my acceptance letter. So, off to college in the fall. I had all summer to dread it!

Telling my kids was a real chore. They could not believe I was even thinking about college. I just knew they had visions of this old lady on campus running around with polyester pants. Cara was living in South Carolina, and Becca and Alena were in Fresno. Phillip was living with Fred in Salinas. I settled in on campus in a dorm into which Alena and Phillip moved me.

We pulled up to the parking lot. I saw all these big dorms, and I was on the 4th floor. I saw a dreaded look on Alena's face. I had to put on a few clothes to get up to the top. So we got a cart, and up the elevator we went. Walking into my first dorm apartment was nice, with two bedrooms, a kitchen, living room, and one bathroom.

I was coming to the end of my first year of my bachelor's. I found myself in a tizzy as I needed to find an internship for my major. Internships require you to go to a place off campus where you work half time to get experience for the major you have chosen. The biggest holdback was my disability. Parking was very expensive. So it would be difficult to go into town. So, as it was, I was changing parking every two hours, or you were ticketed in the city. Prayed for something to happen. Then the next day, I went to our dean of social work, and asked her to help me. I was upfront about my situation. I found out that it is better to tell the truth in the beginning than to be in a bind later. She said she would think about it, and I left.

In my second year, I was getting tired. Doing nothing but papers every day and sitting on the computer until 3:00 a.m. I once again began to question myself for ever starting college in the first place. I began my little pity party again. The next thing I knew, my phone was ringing. It was the Dean of Social Work asking to see me in her office.

"Linda, I would like you to meet someone who I think may help you in finding your internship". Roma Guy is her name. I made an appointment to see this woman as soon as I could. Time was running out, and I knew that most of the social work students already had their internships chosen.

I walked into Roma's office. She asked me to sit down and explain what I wanted to do in my internship. I knew I wanted to write my first book and work with people with disabilities. I will never forget that day. It was a stressful day for me, as she told me to go home and write exactly how I was going to do my internship in outline form and return it the next day. Needless to say, I was doing a lot of praying because I did not know where to begin. I sat down at my computer and began to write. In 5 hours, I was finished. I had a plan, and it would be implemented on campus.

Returning to Roma's office the next day, she read my plan. She was pleased and told me she was afraid I would struggle with the project but knew I could do it. Little did I knew this would be the key person to my future of immeasurable favor.

In my life, I never did anything but have kids, take care of them, and try to get a better job, paying more every time I moved up. This was all done "before I had brain surgery".

Why would I have to go through all of that just for this? Little did I know there were more hurdles to go through.

After leaving the grocery store on Monday, I was driving back to campus. I was about to turn and could see the university from where the stop light was. As I began to slow down, l looked up and saw a truck coming up from behind me. I thought, "Linda brace yourself this guy is not going to stop! About that time, I felt the impact. The car in front of me was already stopped, and I was just stopping. My car was crunching in between the two vehicles. The man behind me was going about 45 mph. People from all sides began to run to my car, thinking I might be gone, but there I was sitting in a fetal position behind the wheel. Not a scratch on me, I walked out, thanking God for my life. The other two cars were not as lucky. They went to the hospital, but they were fine. I was fortunate.

Now, I had to get busy with insurance companies and finding another car. It seemed as if things kept getting in my way. I could not understand this, as it felt like two steps forward and three back. I needed to get to my subsequent lesson before locating a loaner vehicle to travel to Salinas. I was so thankful for those weekend trips. It was always a much-needed break.

Getting a nice car was so much fun! It was a black Chevy. I love my cars so much that I was almost ashamed. It was the end of the first year, and I was beginning to look forward to the summer. I would go and visit Cara (my daughter) and her three children in South Carolina. I took one class in the summer in order to be able to breathe when classes started again. I had the internship to look forward to, and I was ready for a break.

Walking into the administration office, I saw a woman with whom I had become acquainted.

I told her how I was flying to South Carolina to see my daughter and was looking for a place to keep my car while I was gone. She told me that I could park it at her house in the city, and that way I would not have to pay parking or have it moved every two hours. That would really help me out. I took her car, dropped it off, and left the next day for a summer trip with my girls. San Francisco Airport was always busy and filled with exceptionally interesting people. If you were lucky, you might see an occasional movie star.

Summers with the children were always great. The grandkids were growing up, and I missed them so much. We had always been close, especially since my surgery. I think I called Cara every day to check to make sure the kids were doing well.

My vacation lasted 4 weeks, and it was time to go home after a wonderful time with the family. I reached the San Francisco airport and went to the dorm by airbus. When I reached my room, I saw my phone flashing with a message. turned it on, and it said, "Hi Linda, this is Donna. I need to talk to you as soon as possible." This was the woman who allowed me to park my car at her residence while I was on vacation. Even though I was a little taken aback, I called right away. To cut a long tale short, she fell in her home while I was away and was unable to get into her pickup to go to the hospital. She therefore stole my automobile. She hit a pole on the way and totaled my stunning black automobile. Without it, I could not survive. What I was hearing just blew my mind! The lesson to be learned from this story is to not love something so passionately that you can never imagine losing it because you will!

So, again, I went car hunting. The difference between this time and the last is that I found a car that I could live without!

The second semester of my bachelor's was the most exciting time of my life. I did so many things that it would take too long to name them. To start, my mentor, Roma Guy, helped me write my first book. She enrolled me in a class for the homeless. This class was very interesting, I really did not know that much about homelessness. But how about going out on the streets of San Francisco to hang out? That was exactly what the first assignment was. This was a computer class, and everyone would meet once a week to discuss their findings. I was amazed at what I learned.

Walking downtown San Francisco can be a treat in some areas, but in others, not so much. The homeless district is filled with people who have nowhere to live but the streets. They push carts and wear dirty clothes. Some of them are mentally ill and not on medication. It is not a pretty sight. I was to choose one person, get to know them, and take them to lunch. This was a difficult assignment because, walking down the street, everyone wanted to know you. I had one particular lady with a big straw hat and a long quilt-like dress say, "Hey you! Come over here!" She led me to a side alley where we could talk. "I haven't seen you around here before!" "No, you haven't", I said. 'My name is Betsie", she said. We seemed to get along fine, as she was an older woman about my age. There was a McDonald's about two blocks away, and when I asked if she would like to have some lunch, she looked down at her clothes and said "I haven't fit to be seen with you in this." I assured her that she was just fine. When we walked in, I was not surprised at the disapproving glances and whispers among the others. I told Betsie to sit down and I would get her lunch. I returned with a cheeseburger, fries, and a coke. Betsie ate like she had not had food in days. I let her finish her lunch, and as I sat there looking at this woman, I began to think. This is someone's daughter, maybe a mother, aunt, or sister. I felt pain in the depths of my soul. As we began to talk, I learned things I thought were impossible. Betsie was a college graduate. She became disabled and was unable to work. She filed for disability, and no one would take her in until she started receiving her money. The streets became her home, and now she makes the same kind of friends. Her life is now comfortable, and she does not need to be put somewhere to be anyone except who she wants to beBetsie taught me a lot that day. We cannot evaluate people solely based on their outward appearance. We became friends, and up until I graduated from college, we had lunch together every week.

In this homelessness class, I was also able to speak to students on campus who were living in their cars and going to college. They did not have the money for an apartment. I was put in some pretty interesting situations.

One day, as I was sitting at my desk in my dorm room, a call came from the Dean of Social Work. The school of social work was sending me a recommendation to the Masters' Program at San Francisco State and hoping I would accept. This was a real challenge, as I did not think I could stay another year without Phillip, my son, being close to me. I was truly surprised by this request. I began to think about another universities I could attend. I called State Rehabilitation, and they were willing to put me through to my master's program as I had shown them I was serious about my educational endeavors. My decision was made to go to Fresno State because my daughter Rebecca lived there, and that is where I could see taking Phillip with me.

I began getting my reference letters together to go to Fresno State starting in the fall of 2001.

Roma Guy was keeping me busy. I was writing a book and going to a class, and now I had started a program on campus called the DEAR program (Disability Education, Action, and Representation). This program provided education, support, and advocacy on campus for students with disabilities. Many students were having problems with professors understanding their disabilities. I could see how this might help students. I began mentoring students and talking with their professors to help fill the gap in understanding. I was also doing presentations on campus regarding disability and was asked to join the student body. I wanted this program to help others understand the importance of accepting oneself after a disability. This was a very successful program, and I was very busy all year with my book, my classes, and my speaking engagements. The school year was about to wrap up, and Roma came to me one day. She told me that I had been nominated for the STAR AWARD (Student's that are Recognized for Outstanding Community Leadership) for the California State University. I was honored, but I did not know what this entailed. She went on to say this award would allow me to fly to the Chancellor's home and have dinner with other students who had also won from other universities. This was such an honor for me to be recognized in this fashion. I hardly knew what to say.

Off I flew to LA. It was a beautiful day. The recognition ceremony was so special, and the outdoor dinner was lavish, with chefs in white hats. I accepted my award, and the Chancellor spoke about my work on campus. This was a great honor and one I will never forget. The next day was Ceasar Chavez Day, and we all went to work on some of the grounds in his honor. It was back to school and time to get ready for graduation and the finishing of my book.

A phone call came a few weeks later from the San Francisco Chronicle. They wanted to do an article on me for the paper with a picture. Again, I was honored. They shot the picture in my dorm room with my graduation gown and hat. I held the hat over my heart. God is so good. I was asked to give a presentation and play the piano for my 2002 graduation. This was the greatest honor, as I had the privilege of telling all parents that their children are an investment. If you invest in them, they will, in turn, invest in you. I was able to say that my story was a little different. My children invested in me, and now I will invest in them. If it were not for my children nursing me back to health with their unconditional love, I would not have been there to give that speech, play the piano, or earn my bachelor's in social work. Roma Guy was a very special person in my life's journey. She was the one who sent me on my way!

Everyone, in my opinion, has that one person that motivates them, inspires them, and gives them the assurance that they have what it takes to succeed. Every Saturday, I continued to call my mother. "Now, Linda, you realize that all this trouble and time was in vain. What will you do after you leave that place? You won't get a job, ever! All of them desire having guys labor for them. I had grown accustomed to my mother's criticism by this point, but I was ready to show her that she was mistaken.

My year ended with the realization that it was a year of great favor, and little did I know that it would continue for the next two years.

Face It

I was accepted to Fresno State for the fall of 2001. It was different than San Francisco. The main two streets of Fresno, Calif., are Shaw and Blackstone. If you know those streets, you can get almost anywhere in the city. I realized that this was my kind of city. Only two directions to worry about! I started living with my daughter and her husband and then found an apartment that made me feel like I was on a tropical vacation in Hawaii all year. My balcony overlooked palm trees and a big, beautiful blue swimming pool. I was meeting more new people and learning so many new things. Disability was more embraced at California State Fresno University, and I did not have the problems I did at San Francisco State. Two of my professors, who were my mentors, had a disability, and one of them taught a disability class. I felt more at ease in Fresno because I lived just down the street from the university, and it was easy to find my way on the streets of Fresno.

Now let me tell you. Fresno, California, is hot in the summer. I parked my car that day in the student parking lot. I put my ticket on the dashboard and left for about an hour. I came back to pay my ticket, and it was burned to ashes on my dash! I would have to learn to deal with this heat. It was not San Francisco.

I was in the process of looking into getting Phillip (my son) to Fresno. There were some apartments through Mental Health that I had looked at. My classes at Fresno State were much more intense. I did not know if I could have Phillip with me and do the work for school that it demanded. I would have to do two years of internships, and one year would be spent doing my thesis.

On campus, I noticed there were not a lot of programs for people with disabilities. I was looking to start something but was not sure how to go about it. I decided to implement it into my internship, as I did at San Francisco State. I called it "PBWD: Professional Business Women with Disabilities." I made a brochure and began to advertise on campus for a group to meet every two weeks. This program was very successful, as there were so many professionals going to school with disabilities. Some were unseen, such as acquired brain injuries, back injuries, hearing impairments and many more. Our meetings were successful, and we had a fashion show on campus. Most of the women in the group were professionals and leaders in the community. We called the press, and they came and did a write-up on me and the group. I was amazed at what was happening and knew it was not me doing all this but a higher power much greater than myself. I The Fresno Bee News did a segment in their paper about me and the program. Later, the mayor of Salinas called me in and presented me with an award.

My first book, "Under the Weeping Willow Tree," was finished in 2002. I knew this book could not be published until my mother had passed. She would not have been happy with some of the things I wrote, and she would not have understood them from her perspective. I now know, having grown up, that she did her very best as a stepmother. She did what she thought was best for me. I do accept that. My mother passed away two years ago, in February. I knew now was the time to finish and publish my first book, "Under the Weeping Willow Tree".

The internship at the Independent Living Center in Fresno offered me a way to work more on the campus group and to do more outreach in the community. I did not know I would hit some hurdles while there.

One day after finishing my brochure on professional business with disabilities, one of the men walked in and told me it was very unprofessional. I was really taken aback by all his negativity! (That was a little too close to home for comfort.) And my pride was a little hurt too. That incident made me take a closer look at my work and do a better job. Everything I put out in the community was always edited by a professor. Too bad I had not read Ron Carpenter's book "The Necessity of an Enemy". (Carpenter, Ron, 2012) It would have saved me all the sulking I did after that incident.

I really did not learn a lot from this internship, but it offered me a lot of time to work on my program, which kept me busy along with so much school work. I was able to meet a lot of people who spurred me on in program planning and development with PBWD. (Professional Business Women with Disabilities)

My second year of my Masters' Program was very challenging, as I was writing my Master Thesis on "The Influence of Psychosocial and Spiritual Realms on Professional Women." As I started my internship with the Cancer Society, this gave me more practice with my group work with those with cancer. I was able to do some groups with parents of children who had cancer and those who were terminal. At the end of my internship, I was also able to write a manuscript for the American Cancer Society's Policies and Procedures for future interns.

Phillip, my son, had already moved in with me. It was a great experience for me to have him. However, at times, it was also stressful.

"Mom," I would hear about 2:00-3:00 a.m. after I was deep in sleep. "Could you come and let's talk?" Sometimes Phil would have to talk his feelings out to help him process.

However, I had a 7:00 a.m. class, and I knew how I would feel the next day. I learned that sometimes in life, it is not all about you. My son is a very important person to me, and he did come first. I knew the importance of talking to him, and I did what any mother should. I got up! We also had our trials with disability. One month he would get his Social Security, and the next they would cut him off for no reason. I was on Social Security Disability during my master's, which helped me to be able to not work and go to school. But I had to get an attorney at one point to get his social security back. The system is difficult to maneuver. I really did not want to deal with it, but it was necessary. I went down to the Social Security office in Fresno to see what the problem was. The problem was that they had the wrong social security number for my son. They changed it, and he started receiving disability benefits again. This is why having an advocate is so important. If there is no one to speak for you, it can cause a very big loss to you in the end.

The second year of my master's was very eventful. I was able to finish my book and learn a little more about the organizations. When you come to the end of your master's, it is all about the thesis. I was doing group work and some focus groups, along with continuing my group and numerous papers. I was too far gone to look back, and I knew I had reached my purpose on some level. I wasn't actually sure what that purpose was. I just kept moving on.

Next page: "Elementary Isn't College"

I was just about to reach the end of my road. I was ready and driven. and no one was going to stop me. I had come too far and worked too hard for that. However, there was one more hurdle to go through, and of course there would be more, but probably not like this one.

One afternoon in our Social Work with Organizations class, our professor asked us to pass our papers to the front, and he was going to have another student grade our papers. Well, I already thought this was not a good idea. Most students are critical and biased. It would not be so bad if you had some constructive criticism. So, at the next class, everyone was to give the professor the other student's paper that they had graded with a short paragraph of what they thought. Then, they were to go to the person they graded to talk about what they thought.

I was miffed. I sat in my seat, and no one was coming to my desk to say anything to me about my paper. I waited until after class, when everyone was gone, and told the professor that my colleague had not come to me about my paper. He also looked confused as he shuffled through the stack until he came to mine. He had this strange look on his face, and then he turned to me and said, "Linda, this student says that this paper you wrote is elementary school writing." I looked at him in awe. I was speechless, and so was he. Then he said," I would like to take a few minutes to read this." When he finished, he looked at me and said," I will get to the meaning of this, because this is an "A" paper." I was still taken aback by the whole situation. This student (you know who you are) did not attend the last classes of the semester. I was beginning to wonder if she was going to go to graduation!

I have heard about people like this. I get sermons about this all the time. It is called "favor haters". And they usually get what God has for them in the end. Just like this one did.

On the day of my master's graduation, we were all in line, ready to go. I walked in with the professors and set up on the front row of the stage. This was because I was playing piano for my graduation. Not many even knew that I could play. I can remember sitting down on the piano bench, and as I did, I looked at this young lady right in the eyes and smiled. You see, this is not elementary. It took a long time and a lot of hard work and perseverance to learn this and get where I was on that day. If nothing else, it showed her that you cannot judge anyone by what you think. Always remember, "He (God) knew you before you were ever made". He put the right stuff in you to make you who you are and are becoming. No one can take that from you, ever.

That was my last hurdle in school, anyway. Now it was time to celebrate!

My graduation dinner was so beautiful. I had it catered and invited speakers. Of course, Roma Guy was one of them. She was the highlight. And then, the President of the American Cancer Society was there, as were my professor for disability, my mother, brother, children, and the women who attended my PBWD (Professional Business Women with Disabilities). My grandson, Shayne, wrote a song he played on the guitar for me, and my little granddaughter sang a song. It was wonderful to give praise to those who helped me through the last 7 years of college. It was truly an honor. I then took my family for a week to Yosemite to celebrate together. It was a great occasion that I will never forget.

However, now I knew it was on to more serious things, like getting a job, finding out where I should live, and getting to know me after I had been a student for so long. I really felt I could not do anything but be a student.

A Long Overdue Conversation

It was wonderful being with my family after this accomplishment. But there was one more thing that had to be considered. My mother. You know, the woman named "Dorothy". She actually did not realize what all this meant to me. As she sat at my master's graduation, she looked at me with a look that I could not interpret. It could have been one of disbelief or distaste. I was for sure, but that night was the night of "the talk". A very serious one that I know she would have rather not heard. And I learned more than I wanted to. This conversation brought more clarity to me than I thought was possible.

Mom, you know I have always felt like you thought I was just plain "stupid". I have lived my whole life for you. I married men because you said I should. I wore the clothes you said I looked best in. I played piano because you wanted me to be a preacher's wife, and I did all this to make you happy. I accomplished all those things for you. But, still, I do not feel worthy of your blessing or think you see my value as a person. As my mother looked at me with tears in her eyes, she said, "I think it was because I have never felt worthy of anyone's love. You see, as a little girl, I was sexually abused. I bore the shame alone for all these years. I could never speak of the shame or the loss of my childhood. I have loved you, but I have lived my life through you. I know this was wrong, but I have loved you. That night, I learned a great secret and the reason why my childhood was so harsh and protected. As my mother lay crying in my arms that night, we reacquainted ourselves. I wish this had been done years ago. It could have spared a lot of heartache and pain. One must not forget that there is a time and a season for everything.

It Takes One to Know One

I decided to move Fresno back to Salinas, California. I stayed with my friend Suzanne for a while, and I was with Fred for a while. Cara's family moved to South Carolina along with Alena. Becca stayed in Fresno, and Phil was again staying with Fred. Fred and I were not getting along, and I moved to a townhouse in the city. I was trying to figure out what I could do in social work. There are so many things and directions I could go. I put out applications and was accepted at Hospice in San Jose. Now THAT is where I felt I belonged. It was so wonderful working with families and their children who were losing a loved one, plus I was also working with the person at the end of their life. It was truly a blessing. That is, until it was taking me 2 hours to get to work because of the traffic. I decided to look for a job closer to home. I was contacted by CHOMP (Community Hospital of the Monterey Peninsula Hospice in Monterey). I began working and loved it. I felt this must be where I belong! Then a change came in the hospital, where they were only taking a few people for the hospice project. I was amazed once again, as I was one of the people chosen. I began working and felt good about what I was doing.

While working for hospice, I became acquainted with a family whose son was dying from a brain tumor. Now let me tell you. This was reality at its best for me. As I connected with him regarding his life, I was able to talk to him about his relationship to God and how he felt he made a difference. He was a diamond dealer who was very well off and had made a good life for himself. However, he had dated a girl who he loved, and he had not treated her right. He felt terribly guilty, as she wanted to marry him and he didn't. He asked me to try to find her for him. So, he could say "goodbye". We knew he only had about four weeks to live. His parents were also with him and caring for him while hospice was coming to his home. I worked very hard trying to find her, but it was to no avail. I thought it was a shame that he waited until now to know that he should have married this girl he loved, and he felt the same. Michael found comfort in my presence, as he knew I had had a brain tumor. One night at 3:00 a.m., his mother called me. She said that Michael was asking for me to come. Well, I am his social worker, and I know that when you are dying, you want comfort. I did not think twice about going to their home. I was close to the whole family. When I arrived, it was quiet. Michael was in his bed. I walked over, and he took my hand and said, "It is time, but I had to say thank you for being here for me now and since I learned of my tumor." You brought a comforting spirit and supported my family." He smiled and took his last breath. No one knows the reward you feel after you have given your time, care, support, and love to someone who is going to die.

Going to work the next day, I was called into the office. Linda, I heard you were at the York house last night when Michael died. Is that correct? "Yes!" I said. Well, then you will be reprimanded for this, as you should have called the office. I just shook my head Because, once again, those professionals proved to be cruel. The only difference is that I am now one of them. Speaking my mind, I asked if she would have liked me to call her at 3:00 a.m. or if she had refused anyone who called her on their death bed? She did not answer, nor was I sanctioned for this event.

Working for hospice was a wonderful experience, but it was part-time. So I went to work on the side as a school social worker. Now, I was getting a lot of experience in social work as I was working with hospice, children, and teachers in the schools. There are definitely stories to be told about these jobs. I found that I preferred hospice.

Cara called me one day about my granddaughter, Alyce, being sick. She had a condition where the blood vessels would rise to her skin. She was very sick. I was always close to her, and I began making plans to move to South Carolina. I made my plans. Phillip was already with me again, as were my daughter Alena and her husband. We decided we could caravan. This would be a new experience for me, as I was going south across the world. I had been to the south, but I really did not get out as I was always visiting the grandchildren.

I decided to have a garage sale and sell everything I had so I could have the money to live on for a while after I moved. Alena and I began to get things prepared for the sale. I remember how hard it was to let go of so many memories. In the car, I packed my suitcase, my home decorations for the walls, and all of my books from college. I had $4000.00 in my pocket, and I was on my way to South Carolina. I was not sure what I would find there, but I knew if my girls and grandchildren were there, that was where I wanted to be.

A Sad Goodbye To A New Beginning

I remember Fred's face when I went to say "goodbye". To the man I had been. I knew that our lives were not going anywhere, and I knew I needed to step out of the box. I was now a different person with dreams, goals, and visions. He felt as if I was taking away a part of his family too. This was very difficult for me, but I knew there would have to be a very big change before we could even be together.

Off we went with two cars from California to South Carolina. I had a Masters ring on my finger and three degrees to hang on the wall. Now, that seemed to me like something was missing. But I pressed on. My faith was with me, and God was by my side.

Cara lived with her husband and three children. We all stayed with them for about two months. I was trying to figure out how to get a job and what to do in the south. I had lived in California for 35 years. I did not know the first thing about the south. Except, "Hi y'all". It was definitely a culture shock, but I found I could fit in almost anywhere. I went out looking for a place to live. Cara and I went to this little double-wide trailer. It was nice enough, and the yard was really big. When we walked in, a man with a suit on was there to meet us. I was really dreading all the explaining I was going to have to do.

This man was the president of a bank. I told him how I was looking for work and had hoped to find it soon. He looked at me and said, "Good, sign right here". Lease with an option to buy. He didn't even ask my name.

Moving in was interesting because there was no refrigerator, stove, or washer and dryer. Alena and her husband were with us. This place had four bedrooms, and I was praying I could pay the rent. We went out and bought a small hot plate and proceeded to make spaghetti, mac and cheese, and a few other things that did not have to be refrigerated. I thought many times, "Is this how someone with a Master's degree is supposed to live?" I felt inadequate and wondered what my children were thinking of me. I prayed every day and at night on my blow-up bed. In the morning, I was sleeping on the floor due to the lack of air.

No one complained. We knew we would struggle, and at the same time, we were getting stronger and becoming better people for it.

One night, while sleeping on the blow-up bed, something woke me up in the middle of the night. It was a strange feeling, like someone was in the room. I immediately turned on the light next to me on the floor. When I did, I could not believe what was right next to me. It was so big that I thought it was going to talk to me. It wasn't a spider, but it had big black eyes, and it looked at me right back. I said to it, "Oh no! You are not taking residence in my room! It measured about 11/2inches and it was round with a soft body covered in fur. I took the biggest college book I had (I knew it would come in handy someday) and held it over my head. I let it fall and heard a "SPLAT". I could not pick that book up for a good two weeks. Welcome to the south! That is probably what he was trying to tell me.

I began to look at some of the local magazines. I did not know anyone except my family. In fact, I felt that I was brought to the south for them. I really did not reach out because I felt fulfilled, except for one thing. I had no church home. I was raised in such a strict environment. I wanted to find somewhere I could feel comfortable and not be hounded by my looks, the way I dressed, or who I was.

One night I had been reading, and I turned on my tiny TV. I flipped through the channels, and I found this preacher who had this southern accent, but there was something different about it. What he was saying made sense. I had not seen the first part of the service or the worship part. I listened to the whole sermon. This was 2005, and he was speaking on "Your Inheritance" I | was so moved that I began searching for this church. I needed to know where I could find it. The TV said it was in Greenville. Well, I did not know where Greenville was, so I went on a map quest. It was not even 20 miles from my house. I was on a mission! The very next Sunday, I was sitting in that service. I knew I was meant to be there at RWOC (Redemption Outreach Center).

So I found my church. Now I have to find a job. I began to put applications in and received a call from the Department of Rehabilitation. This sounded interesting, as I would be working with disabled people. That was really my purpose. Why else did I go through all this? I was hired, and I loved working with people. I knew it was my calling. But one year from the day I was hired, I was called into his office. "Linda, he said, I am sorry, but I need to let you go". I could not believe my ears, as I was just getting into the groove and liking my work. I was also having a home built, which was in itself a miracle! I asked him", Can you tell me why?". And he said with tears in his eyes, "No, I really can't". That was the mystery of it all. He could not tell me why! There was no reason. He said I was one of his best counselors. That is not something you usually say to someone you are letting go of.

I learned a lot at RWOC. When something happens in your life and there is no rhyme or reason, you know it has to be God. I did not know at that time, but I was just being spurred to the next place in my life that would strategically move me to my next level. I went to RWOC, where they offered businesses looking to hire people. I was called from Greenville Tech. I went in, did the essay, and was hired. As an instructor, I was sent around to different places to teach all types of things, from communication to finances and how to build relationships. It was a good match, but then one day I received a call from a place in Columbia that had received my resume two years before. They asked if I was interested in a full-time position as a case manager doing social work. Can you imagine? Doing what I was trained to do! What a concept! I have been with them ever since.

By now, you are probably wondering what any of this has to do with a disability. Well, first, I want all the women in the world to know that it is not what you look like that makes you who you are. God is the one who does that. Faith, love, perseverance, and a willingness to be led by the spirit that tugs at your heart are indications you are on the right track.

I am a woman of emotions. I could let them get out of control at any given moment.

NO, I did not want to go back to school in my late 40's. I did not want to do anything but sit around the house and feel sorry that my face was a mess, and I did not want anyone to look at me. But that little girl inside me came crashing through, telling me, "You can't ever do anything. You have to feel the fear and do it anyway! Your children are depending on you as a role model! God is revealing your purpose. I knew this was all true, but sometimes reality is hard to take. I was a child who was taking a different direction than what God wanted. Every time I knew I was not doing the right thing, he still pulled me back around.

In this world that we live in today, where women are looked at as objects and disrespected, we as women have to stand up. We are individuals who can make a difference in so many lives around us.

The enemy that is arising in your life today, whether it be your neighbor, your co-worker, or your friend, is an indication that something much bigger and greater is just around the corner. My brain surgery was the biggest hurdle I ever had to get over. I never did anything before I had it except be the perfect child who everyone thought was not too smart or bright and had no voice. Back in those days, children were to be seen and not heard. I could do no wrong because I was controlled and did what everyone else wanted. My mother made me think I was perfect in all ways, just by the way I looked.

"Man looks at the outward appearance, but God looks at the heart". That is the scripture I would say over and over in my mind when someone would stare at me. It helped me get through the pain of knowing I was ugly to others. God also showed me that when someone was looking at me, I needed to approach them and say, "You must be wondering what happened to my face?". It gave me the opportunity to heal myself by letting it out and speaking about my surgery.

In doing my group work with women with disabilities, I found that most of these women, who had made something of their lives, had to fight to push through the labels of who people saw on the outside. It was proven by the focus groups that most of the problems they encountered came from their own families. Most families were ashamed of how they looked and wouldn't accept anything but perfection. Maybe it was because they had a limp or only one arm. From a young age, they were taught to hide and not let anyone see them because their infirmities would draw attention. I experienced this in my own family. Every time my mother would see me, she would touch my face and say, "I think it is straightening up a little." She was always aware of my infirmity. This made me painfully aware, too.

Acceptance is a beautiful thing. It calms you and makes you realize you don't have to impress anyone anymore. It matters that you are happy and fulfilled according to your own standards. Women do not find their identity in their work as much as men do. They are nurturers by nature. It has been proven that women will seek empowerment and look for reasons of disability. If you feel you have a purpose, then you should explore all the possibilities and do whatever it takes to make it work for you. Where do your passions lie? Do you need to think about the possibility of more education? Do not let anyone discourage you or say you are incapable of doing what you want to do. There have been many people who have discouraged me from pursuing my dreams. They have said, "Oh, you are a dreamer". You will not have your dream until you visualize it first. You must sit and dream all you want. Put your vision into motion.

I knew a girl whose parents told her she could hear when she was hearing impaired. As a child, she would not answer them. They would scream at her until they were tired and worn out because she would not answer. It was hard for them to accept her imperfections, but she ended up with her Master's in Education, and she is now teaching deaf and hard of hearing classes to children and teaching parents Braille.

In short, what I want every woman to know is that you must take what you have and run with it. We all come from dysfunctional families in some way. Maybe you were abused physically or emotionally, neglected, controlled, manipulated, or made to feel you did not matter in this world by someone you loved. This does not matter. That was then, and this is now. Low self-esteem is very real, and it has to be addressed. It can ruin your life because it immobilizes you and keeps you from finding your purpose in life.

Many people have come to me saying they don't believe in counseling because it is just someone's opinion of what you must do. God works through people to help you understand what can be done to help you recover from your pain.

I realize that no one knows your circumstances except you. It is difficult for a child who is controlled, neglected, or abused to be resilient. It has been proven over and over again. However, resilience comes from within. You were wonderfully made! Embrace it and know you are a unique individual with all kinds of possibilities.

While at the university, I took a disability class. In this class, there were all types of disabilities. One girl had no hands. She felt so despondent and unwanted. Her disability made her ashamed. My role was to help her see her uniqueness. One day she came into my office with tears in her eyes and asked, "Why am I even here?" We sat down for a little chat. By the end of that semester, she was painting with her toes. She was so talented, and what an artist she was!

Joe, a boy in the class, could not be understood because he stuttered. He came to me with such low self-esteem, and it was difficult for him to speak in class. When Joe talked, people became impatient, just waiting for him to finish his sentence. Together, we came up with a solution. When Joe raises his hand, he walks to the board and writes. He was a natural, and I thought he had taken a creative writing class. Joe began to take a small notebook with him, and when he saw people becoming impatient waiting for his sentence to finish, he just took out his notepad and began to write his sentence. Joe became a writer!

The idea is not to do this for other people; it is to accommodate yourself to make you feel more comfortable and accept your own disability. That goes along with my paradigm of the "Circle of Acceptance." As you accept yourself, others will accept you for your uniqueness, and you will in turn accept your individuality. If you feel comfortable with yourself, others will feel comfortable around you. This is not to say that you need to overdue it. You cannot draw attention to yourself by being overly confident, loud, or narcissistic. No one likes a braggart or someone who shows off. Learn to be who you are. A person who others see as real and confident in the person who God made.

Many people will, sometime in their lives, come face-to-face with disability. You may not even think about it or want to address it. However, everyone has had it touch their lives in some way. Possibly a friend or family member has a disability. The way you know how to approach disability is in the way you approach these people. Do you feel sorry, ashamed to be seen with them, or even afraid to be with them? This is how you will feel if disability comes into your life. Addressing your thoughts and feelings about this now will help you in the event that disability touches you in some way in the future.

This book was written to help others who might have thought they had no chance to make a difference or were immobilized by low self-esteem or issues stemming from their pasts. These are all considered disabilities because they keep you from being your authentic self.

References

The Counseling Corner (2001): Orlando and Central Florida Http://counselingcorner.net/parents/grief.html.

Ackerman-Foster, J. (2006) Obesity and Weight Management, Case Western Reserve, Net Wellness (p. 1) http://www.org/healthtopics/obesity/childhoodobesity/cfm

Heins, M. (1989), ParentkidsRight. Lecture 6, Arizona Daly Star. http://www.parentkidsright.com

Newberg, A. (Neuroscientist), The Wiktionary Encyclopedia (2006) htt://www.wiktionary.org/

Newman, J., and Newman, P. (1999), Development through Life (7th ed.). Belmont, C.A. Brookes, Cole, and Wadsworth (p. 317)

Newberg, A. (Neuroscientist), The Wiktionary Encyclopedia (2006). http://www.wiktionary.org/

Tennov, D., The Wiktionary Encyclopedia (2006) http://www.wikionary.org/

Fortunately for the reading public, Linda Madison is a poetic survivor, bringing pictures of old- fashioned sweat and tears to life in modern-day America. Under the Weeping Willow Tree gave me permission to feel the horror and clarity of courage, the confusion from physical and emotional frailty, not from one's own choosing. Her words are pictures seeded with old-fashioned sweat and tears. Learning and seeking for her is living today for tomorrow, though not just any old day of the week. Linda knows that on any given day, as a single mother of four, she has enough bread on the table and another day she does not; she knows that one day you take your baby to the doctor for care and another day they take you.

Imagine yourself sitting beneath a weeping willow tree, listening, embraced by its shimmering gray-green leaves and drooping summer branches. Enveloped in Linda Madison's tale, true and not to be believed, yet, as you read, her journey, as is yours, is all there in flickering detail, swaying as life happens and bending to the outrageous.

Beautifully rooted, reading Weeping Willow Tree will nourish your day and your week. Give yourself the opportunity to deepen your own wonder. Read it.

Roma P. Guy, M.S.W.
Health Commissioner, City and County of San Francisco,
California Chair, Health Committee,
California Women's Agenda, San Francisco

"Fortunately for the reading public, Linda Madison is a poetic survivor, bringing pictures of old- fashioned sweat and tears to life in modern-day America. Under the Weeping Willow Tree gave me permission to feel the horror and clarity of courage, the confusion from physical and emotional frailty, not from one's own choosing. . . Learning and seeking for her is living today for tomorrow, though, not just any old day of the week. Linda knows that on any given day as a single mother of four she might have enough bread on the table, and another day she might not; she knows that one day you take your baby to the doctor for care, and another day they take you. Imagine yourself sitting beneath a weeping willow tree, listening, embraced by its shimmering, gray-green leaves and drooping summer branches, enveloped in Linda Madison's tale, true and not to be believed. . . Beautifully rooted, reading Under the Weeping Willow Tree will nourish you day and your week. Give yourself the opening to deepen to your own wonder."

Roma Guy, MSW;
Previous Health Commissioner, City and County of San Francisco;
California Chair, Health Committee,
California Women's Agenda San Francisco

Linda Madison holds a master's degree in social work and works for Columbia Health Care in Columbia, South Carolina. She works with all populations that have disabilities.

She survived a seventeen-hour brain surgery and understands the grief and loss of women who have had tragic events in their lives. Through this experience, she learned to accept a life after disability.

Linda now lives in Easley, South Carolina, where she enjoys life with her children, and her grandchildren. Playing piano continues to be her solace during devotion as she prays and meditates daily.

Cara, Linda's daughter, passed away at age 51. Tye, and family, and Alyce live in Easley, SC. Shayne and his family live in Kansas City. Rebecca lives in Easley, South Carolina; Phillip and his mother, Linda, also live in Easley.

The past experiences of death, grief, and loss have made our family aware that every moment must be appreciated and lived to the fullest.

In Loving Memory of Cara Lynee Hare Reyes

Date of Birth
March 21, 1970

Date of Death
October 7, 2021

Cara Remembered and Honored
4:00pm

A Difficult and Rewarding Year

Many years have passed since I finished my book. There have been births, surgeries, marriages, deaths, and many other interruptions in life. I lost my stepmother (Dorothy) and my sister, Marsha. These were difficult times, but nothing compared to what I would have to survive next in my life.

It was October 7, 2021. I can remember my steps so vividly that morning, as I had just awakened. As I methodically moved about in the morning, drinking my daily cup of coffee and taking my morning meds, I was startled by my phone ringing. I answered my phone, "Hello, I said" A shaking voice at the other end said, "Mom, she is gone." It was my son-in-law regarding Cara. I can only remember the pain I felt as I screamed "NO". I will be right there." She lived only a few minutes from my house, but everything I did during that phone call was a blur. I don't remember what I wore or if I even combed my hair. It was a call a mother never wants to receive at any time of the day.

In just a few short months before, I had just had one hip replacement and was waiting to get the second in a few months. I was having a difficult time getting around. I was still on my walker (which I hated). I wondered how I was going to do this. Driving up the driveway to the house, I saw other cars parked. I got my walker out, and I proceeded up the driveway. As I entered the house, there was a hush, a feeling that was so familiar to me as I worked for Hospice as a social worker. Turning the corner, I saw my sweet, loving daughter lying there in the arms of her husband. I wanted too much to lay beside her, to touch her, to talk to her, and to tell her I loved her. But I could not get down because of my hips, and her husband was cradling her. This was her greatest love. Fernando was his name.

The pain I felt was unbearable. "How could this happen?" I said to myself. Cara had been sick for many years, and no one could put a finger on the problem. She went from to having fibromyalgia to lung problems and breathing disorders. As a mother, I watched her suffer in silence, doing things she was unable to do without complaining.

Two weeks before, she had come to my home to stay for three days after knee surgery. Those were the most cherished times I will never forget. She called me Mama. "Now, when you have that hip surgery, Mama, I will come and take care of you". She was always a giving and caring person who loved with all her heart. On our mother-daughter get-togethers, Mc Donald's was the place we ventured. The menu was a cheeseburger and caramel frape. She was an excellent mother, always there and homeschooling the children daily.

This was a very trying time for Phillip, as he and his sister were very close. Schizophrenia was already taking a toll on him, and this magnified his condition of sleeplessness and depression. I feared for him and what he was going through. Family and friends gathered at the funeral home to pay their respects, and there I was, on my walker and wearing the hat Cara always wanted me to wear, but I never did. Isn't it funny how we are sad to think about the things we didn't do and should have. Now it's too late.

It was difficult to play piano for this event (the funeral), but I did. A song I had played for her a week before (In the Garden). It was so appropriate, but difficult. However, it was not more difficult than it was for her father to be the featured speaker. I had been married to him over 40 years ago, and I could just imagine all the memories he had of Cara as she reached womanhood. We were blessed to have her with us for 51 years. She had a heart attack.

Days passed, and I prayed for peace and comfort. Me, Phillip, Becca, and Lena weathered the storm of someone passing who you loved so much. You never forget the wonderful memories, but the void in the heart of a mother is a hole that remains unfilled. Memories of her playing with her dolls, times of adolescence, her smile, and the way she made me feel when she hugged me are always vivid in my mind. *The love we shared was deep and never to be forgotten.*

Angels From Heaven

One day, checking through my phone, I came across a message I had from ancestary.com. A man had written to me named Tim. He said in the text that he believed he was my cousin. I thought, *Well, I have about 900 of those on my ancestry*. But something told me to write him back. We started communicating and sharing with our relatives. The deeper we checked, the more we found out that he was not my cousin but my nephew! Apparently, my biological mother, Earlene, had a child in her teens that she gave up for adoption. This was so amazing to me because no one ever mentioned it. I am the last of the Parrot's in my biological mother's family living, so this was amazing that they even found me! I had an older sister named Yvonne. Her children were my nieces and nephews. I was so overjoyed to know I had more family. We continued to connect over the next few months, and they made plans to come and see their new aunt. My older sister, whom I had never met, passed away just a few years ago. I was saddened to know I missed the opportunity to know her. In finding this wonderful adventure of a new family, I felt this was a gift from above. God knew the unbearable pain I experienced from losing Cara, and to have family in my life that I never dreamed of was a blessing from heaven.

Our visit was as if I had known them all my life, and there were so many similarities in our families. She had even named one of her children "Linda," and one of her children, a daughter, had passed away at around Cara's age.

It is ironic that this book was written for my children, and especially for Cara. I wanted her to know how much I appreciated her love and devotion to me during and after my brain surgeries. I thought it as a memory for her when I was gone. I learned a great lesson from this. A person can never be sure what tomorrow holds. Every day is a gift. You should never take for granted what you have today, as it can be gone tomorrow. Every person is of great value, if not to you, then to others.

Sitting at my desk, I am on my way to another chapter in my life. Another day in the life of a professional woman with a disability. Living to show others how they too can live with a disability through difficult and strenuous circumstances, growing and developing their character, and loving who they have become. No, it is not easy. It takes time, but it is attainable. The choice is always yours. "Feel the Fear and Do It Anyway" by Susan Jeffers, Ph.D. It will be well worth it wherever your journey takes you, as long as you stay focused and driven to find your individual reason for being in the place that was chosen for you!

"A Constant Companion"

You came to me like a
Thief in the night
Unexpected, unwanted
You took away my pride.
You stripped me of my self-esteem
My smile,
I wanted to die.

Rejection, anger, denial,
Was all I had
You took away my identity.
Who was I and who are you?
"I am your Constant Companion,"
You said. I will never leave you.

In my pain, you comforted me
You challenged me to look beyond
The outside
I looked within.
I found love, joy, and peace in having Life.
I found myself, I found you,
My constant companion,
My disability.

By Linda S. Madison

www.ingramcontent.com/pod-product-compliance
Ingram Content Group UK Ltd.
Pitfield, Milton Keynes, MK11 3LW, UK
UKHW041852190726
13854UKWH00002B/860

9 798330 232291